*In the end it was too much
Like looking in the mirror
And I had outgrown myself*

— Lydia *Nitya* Griffith

What is Yoga?

Many people view Yoga in the gym format, as an exercise. Yet, Yoga is a path, a spiritual path, and there are ministers of Yoga who've devoted their lives in service to this philosophy. Reading *The Yoga Sutras of Patanjali* translation by Sri Swami Satchidananda illuminates clearly that though Yoga may not be considered a religion, it is most definitely a lifestyle.

Living the Yogic path is as beautiful as any religious or spiritual path that awakens in you a sense of deep compassion, love, and respect for all living creatures. It's a way of non-violence, of truthfulness, of sharing in every imaginable way, and of kindness to others without discrimination. Hatha Yoga includes the *asanas* (physical movements or poses), *pranayama* (breathing practices), *Yoga nidra* (deep relaxation), meditation to still the mind, *kriyas* which are purification processes like neti nasal washing and fasting, and diet which is vegetarian and *sattvic*, meaning closer to the earth—unrefined foods, such as fruits, grains, legumes, veggies, nuts, organic dairy, and water.

So, when you take a Hatha Yoga class and feel all that wonderful, yummy, peaceful goodness as you walk out the door, know that you can continue to develop that level of peace in your life by adopting a more Yogic lifestyle. That's our curriculum each day at the Nitya Living Summer Yoga Camp—we teach children to *live* Yoga.

One camper said, "This is the only place where I can be me and I can think." Mason age 6.

A parent shared, "You have given my children a wonderful gift of spirit and peace. Something I hope will be carried with them for a lifetime."

Musings on Morning Practice

It is early dawn, still dark in the corners of the house
   Where stillness is a blanket to curl into.
Held on a cushion, perched as the owl,
   Seeing clearly with eyes closed.
Breathing in the new day deeply,
   It is from here that everything is possible.
It is from here in this dark, silent stillness
   That you
      Become
      Awake.

It is when we are most busy, most needing our practice, that we often forfeit that one thing that can help most. If you brush your teeth, then you should brush your brain with meditation, rinse your body with Hatha, and floss your breath with pranayama every day. 30 minutes less sleep will not end your world, it will begin it anew. I promise with certainty that your life will become far less stressful if you get up each day for practice.

Start with *pranayama*, some deep breathing, to wake yourself up. Breathe in, filling the abdomen. Carry that breath to your chest, all the way to the collar bone, then exhale through the nose, depressing the chest and collapsing the stomach. Repeat 10 times. Slow, mindful breaths.

Next, choose 4 or 5 *asanas* (poses) that you really love. Hold each pose for a count of 10 slow breaths. Breathe into the stretch; release into the stretch through your breath. Then do two rounds of *Surya Namaskaar* or Sun Salutation.

Lastly is meditation for a minimum of 5 minutes. Take a deep breath in and exhale OM; repeat 2 more times. Feel OM radiate through your body. Focus on the sound of OM moving with your breath. If thoughts come in, just watch them float by like clouds in the sky. Go back to the focus on the breath.

Do not get up and rush into the rest of your day. Take your time, set the pace for your day to be mindful, peaceful, purposeful, easeful and ultimately enjoyable.

Yoga Nidra with a Guided Visualization

Preparation: Tensing & Releasing

Lie flat on your back and close your eyes. This can be on your Yoga mat, on the couch, or even in bed.

Breathe into your legs, hold your breath, and squeeze your legs tight, tight, tight. . . . Exhale, letting them go—*aaaah!*

Now breathe into your hands and make them into fists. Squeeze your arms and hold your breath. . . . Exhale, letting them go—*aaaah!*

Put your hands on your belly and breathe your belly into a big balloon. Bigger, bigger, bigger. . . . Exhale, letting it go—*aaaah!*

Inhaling, shrug your shoulders up to your ears. Exhale, push your shoulders down. Now inhale, wrapping your arms around yourself, giving yourself a big hug, . . . and release. Remember, loving yourself just the way you are is the beginning of loving the whole world just the way it is.

Now rock your head side-to-side. Still your head and wiggle your jaw side-to-side.

Drop your mouth open, inhale, sticking out your tongue. Roll your eyes upward and exhale, making a hissing sound. Now fold it all back up.

Inhale and purse your lips; exhale and let the mouth go.

Now squeeze your face tightly like you just bit into something really sour. Squeeze forehead, eyes, nose, and mouth. Hold your breath, . . . then exhale. Let it go—*aaaah!*

Feel a warm wave of deep relaxation wash over your body. Observe your body still and silent.

Visualization

Now imagine you are a water droplet high up in the clouds. It's winter time and the air is very cold. You begin to freeze and form into a snowflake. You never argued or struggled with becoming a snowflake—you are happy with who you are, just as you are.

Then you, along with billions of other snowflakes, begin to fall from the clouds. Imagine how it feels to be falling—floating, flying, and free. Then you land, and it feels strange to not be free anymore, but to be stuck on the ground, lying with billions of other snowflakes. Then you see how nice it is to be still and silent, happy with who you are, just as you are.

Then a family comes out of a house, and you get rolled into a snowball that gets thrown in the air. You see that you are now part of a fun game. It's also great to feel like you're flying again, even if you are rolled into a tight ball with a bunch of other snowflakes. Then you get rolled into a bigger ball and are now part of a snowman. You are now compressed deep inside the snowman's head, and you're not really a flake anymore. You think at first how strange this is, but everyone in the yard is smiling at you and very happy. You are reminded to just be happy with who you are, just as you are. And if a snow crystal could smile, you are smiling.

But then the day gets warmer and the snowman begins to melt. The snowflakes return to their original form—as drops of water—and sink into the ground. And soon you feel yourself doing the same thing. As a drop of water you roll down what's left of the snowman and sink into the ground. So many water droplets have made a big mud puddle. At first you don't like being dirty, and it all feels very strange, but then some kids come along and jump in the mud puddle and are laughing with delight at the mess they are making. Once more, you feel happy, too—just as you are.

The summer comes and no rain falls for a long time. The mud puddle from the snowman last winter has dried up and the water has become part of the cycle of life. You are no longer a water droplet or a snowflake, but have evaporated into the air; and eventually you shall ascend to the clouds and form a new rain drop. But it really doesn't matter, because no matter what changes happen, no matter how things work out, you are happy with who you are, just as you are.

This story is based on the Yoga term *santosha*, which means contentment, the idea that you are happy with who you are, just as you are, without grasping for more—just content with your life and with yourself.

Pranayama: Are You Breathing?

Prana is Life Force. It is that which propels a rock down a hill. It is the currents coursing through the seas. It is the dance of a kite in the sky. It is the flow of blood through our veins. It is the wind in our lungs. *Prana* is what animates all things. *Yama* is the ability to control, restrain or direct. *Pranayama*, then, is the control of the breath.

Why should we control our breathing? Don't we breathe normally on our own? Well, look at how you are sitting right now. Are your feet on the floor, spine erect, shoulders back, or are you crossed-legged and slouched in your chair? When we sit slouched, with poor posture, we restrict the flow of air coming into the lungs. When our breath is shallow we aren't getting all the oxygen our bodies need to be healthy and to function optimally.

What state of mind are you in? This affects how you breathe as well. Did you run up the stairs to answer the phone a few minutes ago, or get into a heated discussion with a coworker? Maybe you woke up feeling really anxious about a presentation or depressed about a raise you didn't get? Any of these types of scenarios can change the depth and rate of your breathing along with your mind-set.

Why does it matter how we breathe? Many people breathe through their mouth. I call this the "TV breather." Have you ever walked into a room where people are watching TV? They sit wide-eyed, mouth open, slouched in their seats. Sri Swami Satchidananda, founder and spiritual leader of Integral Yoga, said, "The mouth is for eating and the nose is for breathing." The nostrils are designed to purify our air. The hairs in the nostrils filter airborne debris, the mucous secretions in our sinuses capture dust and microbes, and our nasal passages warm and moisten the air as it enters the body. Air entering the mouth is cold and dirty.

Learning to control your breath can play a pivotal role in how your body and mind function. It has been scientifically proven that *pranayama* practices can bring in up to 7 times the oxygen we typically take in a single breath. Some of the benefits include: a more resilient immune system, heightened awareness, greater calm and focus, easing of anxiety and the symptoms of depression, invigoration of the pituitary gland, glowing skin, improvement of symptoms of sinusitis, hay fever, and migraines, plus an overall sense of serenity through the entire body.

Pranayama exercises have been practiced for over 5,000 years. One excellent resource on this subject is the book *Science of Breath* by Swami Rama, Rudolph Ballantine, and Alan Hymes. These practices are simple and can be done anytime.

Dirga Swasam *or the 3-Part Breath*

Begin by sitting with your spine erect, shoulders back (but relaxed), and feet flat on the ground, or in a comfortable, cross-legged position. Exhale completely, pushing out as much air from the lungs as possible, and retracting the abdomen inward towards the spine. The exhalation is crucial, because the more you can empty your lungs, the more you can then fill the lungs.

Inhaling, fill the abdomen like a balloon, then continue bringing in the breath, filling the chest, and finally raising the collar bones.

Exhale, deflating from top to bottom: release the collar bone, relax the chest, and retract the abdomen slowly in towards the spine, until your lungs are empty.

Do 10 repetitions.

Contraindication: If at any time you feel dizzy or light-headed, just stop and try again later.

This breathing practice should be done slowly, mindfully, with total awareness of the movement and control of the breath.

After you've gotten comfortable with the practice, you can lengthen the number of rounds and incorporate this into your daily activities, such as doing the dishes, driving, before going into (or out of) a stressful situation, and meditation. For meditation, I find focus on the breath can deepen and expand the sitting practice in a very rejuvenating, yet calming way.

Nadi Suddhi *or Alternate Nostril Breathing*

Begin in the same posture as for the 3-Part Breath.

Breathing alternately through the nostrils requires closing off one, then the other. This is done by pressing the side of the nose with the side of a finger. If you'd like, use the traditional Yogic hand position, the *Vishnu Mudra* (folding in the middle and pointer fingers leaving the thumb and last two fingers up), or use the pinky and thumb.

Close off the right nostril and exhale through the left; then inhale.

Close off the left nostril and exhale through the right; then inhale.

Continue for 5 rounds (go for 10 if you can).

Finish by placing hands in your lap and doing a deep, 3-Part Breath.

This particular practice balances the left and right sides of the brain and has a calming effect on the nervous system.

You can do this practice when sitting in a traffic jam, a long checkout line, waiting at the doctor's office, before an interview, or other stressful situations. You will feel far more balanced and relaxed after doing alternate nostril breathing.

Stressful situations are a part of life, as is feeling rushed or overwhelmed. Being aware of your breath while practicing *Pranayama* will counter the ill effects of your hectic lifestyle and bring you to a far more serene and controlled state. You will be able to better manage stress, and your body will be able to fight off illness more easily.

The Subtle Body

In the book *The Subtle Body* by Stefanie Syman, I found a passage shared by Alan Watts from the early 1960s in which he recounts a realization he experienced at a gas station. He saw people "pretending not to see that they are avatars of Brahma, Vishnu and Shiva. People who were so good at pretending they're not what they are; they also missed the obvious fact that their bodies were composed of a million cellular gods; that everything that surrounded them, from the gaudy billboards to dust, was numinous, jeweled, unspeakably holy."

It is said in the Buddhist faith that every sentient being is born a Buddha. Anytime you look into the eyes of a baby you can see that Buddha nature. From the time we begin to grasp language, our ego begins to grasp its identity as separate from others. In many ways, we go through our life trying to recapture that initial state of consciousness, that oneness with all, to rein in the ego to truly abide in harmony and interconnectedness.

Our society has sped up considerably since those early days of Yoga in the West. Our ability to be constantly distracted is intense and serves no one's health or well-being. The art of reclaiming that "inner Buddha" or primordial quality is to become still and silent inside. That means you can be in the middle of a meeting, in the middle of a playground, in the middle of an argument, in the middle of a crisis and you can find stillness and quiet within. The art to this, the connecting thread to this, is your breath.

Pranayama or breathing techniques show up in both Yogic and Buddhist practices. This is because it is a fundamental issue in the human condition that we are distracted from realizing who we actually are. You know, when you are not breathing properly, when you feel lethargic during the day, you find yourself sighing, gasping large breaths, or exhaling loudly? The most important aspect of *Pranayama* is awareness. Are you aware that you are breathing? How often do you stop in your day to simply *enjoy* your breath?

Breathe with awareness. Fill the abdomen, then exhale deeply so the abdomen retreats towards the spine. You begin to feel more calm, alert, and refreshed. Now you can find stillness. Now silence can find a place within. The magic that happens over time is that you discover a sense of spaciousness that opens you up to the qualities we all wish to attain—peacefulness, loving-kindness, equanimity, and non-attachment.

Live your authentic self, be the avatar, be god-like, be Buddha-like in how you treat yourself, your family, everyone you know and don't know, whether they are two legged, eight legged or have no legs at all. Why continue to just live the mundane life when you know that your every cell contains these amazing qualities of perfection?

Breathe deeply, and know you are that, and that is Divine.

Cautions for Practicing Hatha

A student once gave me an article published in *Self Magazine* about Yoga injuries.

I was struck by the number of Yoga students who had suffered debilitating injuries mentioned in this article. I also reflected on a conversation I had had with another teacher about the surge of Yoga classes being offered by gyms in which the instructor may not even be a certified Yoga instructor. We talked about the dangers of unqualified instructors, and I emphasized the need for qualified Hatha teachers to educate the masses in what I call "true Yoga." Hmmm . . . *true* Yoga? Yes, not some fitness trend, but the ancient discipline that has traveled over 3,000 years, across the oceans from India to your Yoga mat.

Yoga is rooted in the practice of daily meditation. When you start getting into Yoga, make sure to ask the instructor about learning how to adopt a daily Yoga practice that includes meditation. Ensure meditation is part of the class.

Yoga is non-competitive and that includes with yourself. This is where the Type-A, athletic, go-gettum types can get into trouble. When you push yourself to the edge of anything, you may find you've caused your body injury. Go back to the root—meditation—and start over while leaving your ego on the race track.

Yoga is a mind-body-breath connection in the present moment. Have an awareness of the pose, the movement of breath, and how the body feels in that shape. Take each pose and hold it for as long and as deeply as feels comfortable for your body—not the body on the next mat over, not the body you had 15 years ago—the beautiful body you inhabit at this present moment. And that changes. Some days you can touch your toes, raise up into shoulder stand, do a deep spinal twist, and some days, the body says a loud "NO" of protest. Listen to your body, it is always talking to you.

So let's consider this . . .

Things to Keep in Mind When Taking a Yoga Class

1) **Make sure the instructor is certified** to teach Hatha Yoga.

2) **Ask what style of Hatha Yoga is being taught**, because some styles are far more vigorous while some are more meditative, and others are in very hot environments. You can research the styles of Hatha Yoga online.

MUSINGS FROM THE MAT

3) Always, *always* tell your instructor about any current or prior **physical issues** like migraines, back/neck issues, glaucoma, cataracts, high blood pressure, heart disease, surgeries, sports- or accident-related injuries. If you are more than three months pregnant you should be in a prenatal class. Also, refrain from any inverted poses during your female menses cycle (some traditions of Hatha Yoga abstain from physical exercises during this time of the month).

4) **Be aware that there are *Yoga-like* classes out there** that combine Pilates, acrobatics, or other fitness trends with Yoga poses. These are exercise classes, but not true Hatha Yoga classes.

5) **If you are a beginner, stick with a beginner-level class** for at least three months. Then, if you feel you have a good understanding of the poses, and your body is responding without any strain or discomfort, then go to the next level or to a mixed-level class. There are many students of Yoga who have never moved past the beginner level because it's enough of a practice for them.

I went to visit a Yoga studio as a guest one day. Being an instructor, I felt confident that I could blend into this Intermediate class with no problem. I thought that since I had been practicing Hatha for so many years I could easily do these more challenging poses. I found myself for the first time up in *sirsasana* (head stand). Now, it never occurred to me to think back to my past neck and back injuries from a car accident and my decade of vigorous labor working in a book store. It did occur to me the day after this class when I woke up with intense shoulder and neck ache that lasted for several days after. I recovered without any issue, but I learned a valuable lesson as a student and an instructor: that I should always honor my body first and foremost in every situation. It is because of my own history of back and neck problems that I am hyper-cautious of guiding students into inverted poses like *halasana* (plow) or *sarvangasana* (shoulder stand) and the counter pose of *matsyasana* (fish). Traditionally inverted poses are not introduced until about the fifth class.

The Yoga *asanas* (poses) are the physical aspect of Yoga that brings you to an awareness of your body, mind, and breath in a way that should ultimately lead to a greater sense of ease, peace and health without injury or over-straining. Again, Hatha Yoga is not all about fitness. I highly recommend reading *To Know Yourself* by Sri Swami Satchidananda, the founder and spiritual leader of Integral Yoga, to learn more about how to incorporate all that Yoga is into your life.

Discovering Yin Yoga

The root practice of Yoga is meditation. For me, digging down to the core of Yoga's origin began when I offered to substitute teach a Yin Yoga class. It was obvious, once I looked at the *asanas* and the length of holding each pose, that this initial approach to Yoga was created to support meditation.

During meditation a great deal of strain can be put upon the hips and back if the hips are not open and the back is not strong. Most Hatha Yoga in America is very "yangified"—building up heart rate and muscle tone with a faster pace or intense heat. My Yin teacher, Biff Mithoefer, says, "Intensity is the shadow side of the Healer."

Hot Yoga is often perceived as more "Indian," because, as everyone knows, India can be a very hot place. But Yoga wasn't born in India because meditators were seeking heat. India also borders the freezing cold Himalayas. Yin is by it's very nature a "cool" practice—the counter-balance to "yang" forms of Hatha—because it is slow and abiding. I think Yin has long been overlooked as an option for experiencing Hatha practice and preparing our bodies to support our minds in meditation.

Yin addresses the subtle aspects of the body that tend to get missed: the connective tissues, the joints, and the spiritually-rich connection we can have with our bodies through stillness. During the Yin Yoga practice you are spending about 5 minutes in each *asana*.

As I prepared for subbing this class, I created a sequence of poses and began the practice at home. I found my body drank up the stillness, the sense of releasing and opening as I held *balasana* (child's pose) for several minutes. Then I moved into *hamsasana* (sleeping swan), opening my hips even further. As I held these poses I found a quiet, meditative breath and mind. As an edge would rise up, resisting, the breath and mind allowed the body to slowly, easefully go further.

According to Patanjali, "Yogas citta vritti nirodhah," translates as "The quieting of the fluctuations of the mind-stuff is Yoga." This reminds us of why we practice Yoga in the first place—to abide in our own true nature of peace, free from the harried mind of modern day life. My guru, Sri Swami Satchidananda, always said the goal of Yoga was to attain a peaceful mind, an easeful body, and a useful life devoted to selfless service. Yin Yoga directs you toward that objective by giving you a method designed to ease the body and mind for meditation. With the back strengthened, the hips opened, and the mind focused, I found meditation to be far easier to slip into and hold. The body naturally felt receptive, the mind followed, and my heart opened.

Clearing the Mind

To achieve the meditator's mind you have to get off the fast track spin of the ten thousand thoughts running through your mind at any given moment. To begin meditation you need three things:

Clarity – Calm – Focus

So, in a sense, what you need is a "*Feng Shui* approach" to clearing the mind. There may be time restrictions, personal issues, demands from family, and work stress that have a fist-like grip on your mind. Yet, you know that *you* create your reality. And that can be a hard pill to swallow when you are dealing with something really difficult. Our minds are a cluttered mess of infinite thoughts, desires, dreams, fears, anxieties, and so on. There is a point at which we stop either from exhaustion, illness, or maybe a moment of clarity—a moment at which we realize how our minds and lifestyles are running us through a maze to nowhere good.

Mental clutter can be a lot like waking up on a Saturday morning to realize you haven't done the dishes in a couple days, the laundry basket has thrown up all over the floor, the mail is scattered in piles all over the dining room table, and the more you look around, the more you see a house full of clutter. Your house is very much a mirror of your mind.

This is when it's time to do some *Feng Shui* work inside and outside. When I think of *Feng Shui*, I think of order, flow, and vibrant potential. So, to avoid the weekend cleanup of the house, you could just make an effort to do a little straightening at the end of each day. In the same way you could make an effort to start your day with meditation. Both cleaning and meditation require something of you—commitment. I know, it's a cringeworthy word, but really, why is self-discipline such a chore? Discipline is a way to honor your life by taking time to do the things you *need* to do in order to be a whole, healthy person.

I'm self-disciplined to a fault (I keep my bookshelves organized alphabetically by author and subject). So, when I was in my Yoga teacher training, it was fairly easy for me to adopt a new daily regimen of getting up at 5:00 AM for Hatha Yoga and meditation. Even after I graduated, I maintained my morning date with the Universe, my Self, and my practice. It is my sanity in the midst of my busy life to start my day by *Feng Shui*-ing my mind to be Clear-Calm-Focused.

Get Started:

- **Set a time every day** and honor it.

- **Create a sacred space to practice** where you won't have interruptions.

- **Be there in body, mind, and spirit**, not because you have to, but because you want to, with the purest intentions.

- **Don't be hard on yourself when thoughts come up.** If they are important, write them down. Keep a journal nearby. As you work through your thoughts, you'll find it becomes easier and easier to set them aside and become relatively quiet in your head.

- **Start with a few minutes** and slowly work up to a goal of 30 minutes (or longer, if you prefer).

Know, then, that what you think is what your life will be. There are many people I know who are suffering for various reasons. The more you look at what is causing the suffering, the longer you abide in a painful place. Subtly shift your thoughts from negative to positive. Instead of, "I don't want to be in debt anymore." Try, "I welcome abundance in my life."

Begin to adopt a regular meditation practice. Make time for you to be alone, breathing deeply, letting go of the clutter in your mind, and embracing the brilliant clarity of your true nature.

Experience Clarity-Calm-Focus. A place of peace can be found even in the most hectic life.

Falling Victim to Bad *Feng Shui*

I've been a *Feng Shui* practitioner since 2002, and as much as I'd like to think I've mastered energy like a great cowgirl of the Universal winds, I have to admit I have not. Though, my lasso of knowledge is constantly in motion, attempting to harness the best of a given moment in time, I am not always guaranteed success. Some years this cosmic cowgirl is taken for a ride!

My Chinese astrology for the year may be stellar, but if the *Feng Shui* of my home is awry—*look out*—a duel with the stars is inevitable. With every *Feng Shui* cure in place and every possible décor treatment, I boldly go into each year with great confidence that my fate will overcome and win out the *chi* (energy) of the house. It is a battle I may or may not win. Herein lies the lesson—there are times when we have to surrender to the greater forces around us, for better or worse. Just as every coin has two sides—one side reveals you can do something about it and one side says to surrender and let it go—certainty comes with uncertainty, knowing with the unknown. The beauty of both Chinese astrology and *Feng Shui* is that there is a far clearer understanding of what you're dealing with in the golden corral of life. Is this a real bandito of danger or a mere cowardly villain you can easily overcome? There is a relationship here to be recognized, respected, and nurtured.

A property should be respected as a living organism (if you think about it, buildings eat, breathe, excrete, and have their own personalities). No one can truly own, rent, or lease the Earth. From the lawn to the trees and house, the property vibrates with the natural materials it is made from as well as from how we decorate and furnish it. Your own human vibration along with pets and other living organisms greatly contribute to the energy that resonates either positively or negatively around you. This is the root of what *Feng Shui* is.

Ideally, we all want peace and harmony in our lives. Yoga teaches us that serenity and calm can be achieved through meditation. Yet, how can you feel calm and focused if your home is a mess of clutter, bad energy, or the relationships with it or within it are toxic? As you create peace within your home and peace within your mind, then it only makes sense to also look at how you nourish your body. This brings us to diet. If you run yourself ragged and rarely stop to refuel with *real* food, how can you expect to find peace in your life? Even if you live a balanced lifestyle of work and play, if you eat highly-processed foods—fast food, factory meat and dairy, microwaved meals, re-fined grain products, lots of sugar, lots of salt, junk food, artificial flavors and colors, inorganic preservatives, alcohol, etc.—you are jeopardizing you health. The food industry has done a great job at making food-like products taste really good, but it is not real food. If our bodies are cluttered with unnatural and imbalanced food chemicals, how can we expect our minds to effectively achieve a meditative place of calm?

Your digestive system and other organs of your body will be negatively impacted as well on such a toxic diet. The teaching of *saucha* in Yoga philosophy is to achieve cleanliness and purity in body, mind, and spirit. I've included this *Feng Shui* piece because, to me, it only makes sense that the path of Yoga calls for *saucha*, which means cleanliness and order in one's mind, one's home (and work), and body.

Diet + Meditation + Feng Shui = Serenity and Purity

Feng Shui your home so that you can be the cowgirl or cowboy of your own Energetic Universe! Clean up your diet, clean your mind, clean out your home, and watch yourself shine with renewed vitality!

Riding the Tiger Tail

Riding the flow of energy is what the Tao is all about. Life brings waves of ups and downs.

In business one might experience high revenues one quarter, but the same quarter next year there may be much less. How does one adjust to such fluctuations? How does one budget for times like that? One's social life can suffer setbacks, too—numerous outings with friends and supportive phone calls one season, then suddenly one is alone, feeling isolated, with no one reaching out. Setbacks can be even harder to bear when one embarks on major undertakings, like a home renovation, a career change, or a solemn commitment.

But life doesn't evenly distribute the ups and downs. Sometimes problems come in clusters. If you are met with one delay, loss, or obstacle after another—and nothing seems to be working smoothly—that is a sign to stop, step back, and reassess. Just because you want to be doing something, building something, planning something, does not mean the time is right or you are meant to succeed with that particular endeavor.

In times when things seem obstructed and the energy around you is ebbing, this is a time to do research, planning, self-reflection and meditation. Then slowly begin to reach out and test the waters. Do you get a positive response? Is a friend inviting you out? Is a project you've been planning suddenly finding a time and place to manifest? Then you know you are back in the flow.

Take heed then, if you've been riding the tiger's tail and received a few stripes on your back, to slow it down. Be mindful and aware of how the energy is flowing and master surfing the waves.

Musings on the Moon

Ancient cultures thousands of years ago began following the cycles of the moon to keep time, to understand the seasons and how Nature influences daily life. To know the moon is to know the potency of darkness and the vibrancy of light, to plant seeds on a new moon and to harvest on a full moon.

For over 4,000 years the ancients have celebrated the tradition of the New Year as a welcoming of spring, the return of the growing season, and a time for birth and rebirth. I have become increasingly aware of the subtle, yet profound changes each Chinese Zodiac animal has on our individual lives, on the events of history, on the patterns of Nature herself. As much as I have learned to intuit, study, and predict as an astrologer, there is a part of me that holds space for the great Unknown that is beyond knowing.

Living with the flow of energy—moving forward when the way is open; stepping back when the way is blocked—is the same spirit of the ancients who looked to the moon as a living compass. It is an incredible path to walk in life. The message echoes: be present, be open, be still and silent within, allow for life to unfold just like the cycles of the moon.

Cultivating Heart

The bird-like mind flitters,
Flapping its winged thoughts into the vista.
How can you hold a bird?
How can you hold its wings against its quivering body?
They long to fly—both the bird and the mind.
Soaring high into daydream clouds,
Dipping down into the mire of pessimistic gloom,
Darting in and out of life's trees and brush
does the mind-bird go.
Come into the nest of stillness.
Slow the breath. Close the eyes.
There is a beautiful darkness
Behind the screen of sight and light.
Allow the mind to fold in its winged thoughts
That insist to continue its endless flight.
As you sit with eyes closed and breath calm,
Bring your mind in its luminous stillness
to your heart.
Bring the bird to its nest.
Hold your focus there.
Breathe into your heart and feel love glow,
Expand, and grow.
Love is a sweet elixir
Manifesting from your Heart Nest.
Allow it to seep through every cell
And pore of your being,
And bathe in the Light of your Love.
As you sit, feel Love running off of you,
Pooling into a golden puddle.
Imagine it seeping into the Earth, creating fertile ground
For all of Life to Manifest.

Bring your Love up through the Center of your body
And straight out the top of your head.
Like a beacon, send your Love Light to the Universe,
Blessing all sentient beings.
Cradle your mind like a tiny wren
Into the still radiance of your Heart,
Trusting that as you cultivate this Love with the Universe,
So too are you Loved.

INSPIRED BY A TALK BY
GESHE TENZIN WANGYAL RINPOCHE

Who Are You?

This is a question I ask every day at Yoga camp: "Who are you?"

It's a deep question to ask someone who is 6 or 9 or 14 years old. An adult will answer similarly—saying their name, that they are a boy or a girl, what they do for a living, or what grade level they're in, and at what school. They sometimes state where they live and something about their family. Those answers tell me *where* they are, but nothing about *who* they are.

Who you are is far more interesting.

How you discover that person *inside* of you is through daily meditation, journaling, and Hatha Yoga. Naturally, when you begin such a practice you begin to connect more and more to your *true* Self.

I just finished re-reading the last twenty of my personal journals. I feel blessed that I have chronicled my life since the age of 10. I have had a pretty clear sense of my Self all of my life, and I attribute this to my journaling, which is an intimate relationship between my Self and the pages upon which I navigate self-expression, self-analysis, self-inquiry. Rereading gives me a measure of how far I have come, how much I have learned, how much I have grown. I can see how life has a rhythm of opposites—celebrations and tragedies, depression and resilience, doubt and hope, births and deaths, beginnings and endings, victories and failures. The one constant is me.

We survive because we all yearn to thrive, to experience, to love, and to hold onto that which we covet most dear.

Meditation calms my mind, forces me to be still and listen within. Hatha Yoga allows me to move slowly and easefully in a way that I feel breath and body in union. Journaling is an extension of myself unfolding as I continue to understand my journey, the roles I play, and the people riding along with me.

We never stop answering or asking the question, "Who am I?" We have no beginning or end; we cycle through life's journey ever discovering new aspects about ourselves.

For me, all of my life is made richer with the path of living my Faith. I do not cling or subscribe to one, for they all are a mandala held together by the thread of love.

I am as much a Yogi as a Taoist or an astrologer or a Mother of the Earth. They all inspire me to be my best and to serve.

Who are You? Some of my young Yoga campers one summer responded to this question:

> "I am the horse who gallops in the field restlessly during the twilight. I am the seed who is almost to the surface of the ground just waiting to burst out and become a flower. I am the love that holds two friends together."
>
> —GRACE

> "I am a bird that flys freely. I am a calapiler on a branch. I am a deer that runs freely with joy and happyness. I am a rose that sits and is happy where it is. I am a garden full of fruit that people grow. I am the wind that follows God."
>
> —JULIA

> "I am joy to all the animals in the world. I am plenty of food and water for everybody. I am plenty of homes for young and old. I am the nourishment to all plants and animals in the world. I am the electricity of the world. I am the sun, moon, and stars that shine. I am everything."
>
> —KATIE

> "I am a peace maker, a lover, a karate girl, a yogi, an animal lover, an adventure girl, a mountain goat, a butterfly, a silver stallion, a mother horse giving birth."
>
> —SAVANNAH

The BIG question is, as always, *why* are we here?

And so it was a couple years ago that I found myself at a Yoga retreat, walking back from noon meditation. I had the chant *Om Nama Shivaya* stuck blissfully in my head. I came around the bend in the road, and through the stark fortress of barren winter trees and heavy gray clouds, the sun broke through. It was definitely one of those moments in life that literally stops you in your tracks. For there before me I witnessed the sun prostrating before me on the road. It was as if the Universe had picked me up and lifted free all my burdens. I saw clearly the still lake of emptiness. Tears rolled happily down my cheeks and my heart swelled a love that seeped out my every pore.

Then I heard new words that sang to the same tune as *Om Nama Shivaya* and these words were: "I don't know who I am. I don't know where I go. I am the light that falls on the other side of shadow." Life can do this to us. We can be exalted from the ego-self, the monkey mind, the clutter of our days. It wasn't that I was looking for it, and I didn't cling to it, though its effects have marked my spirit.

There's no drive-thru lane for us to turn down and say, "Yeah. I'll take an order of Enlightenment with a side of Eternal Bliss and World Peace." Nor can we sit on our meditation cushions or walk down our chosen religious path with an expectation of release from *samsara*. The biggest trick to life is carrying the cushion and walking that path everywhere we go—to all people, in all places, in all situations—especially when we are weak and driven by anger, ignorance or attachment.

I inherently know and trust that as long as I hold myself open to possibility, quiet my mind, and still my body, such bliss states will come again to encourage and inspire me in my lifelong quest toward Divine Liberation. Perhaps, the greatest surrendered journey is the one in which there is no Path at all. Then, like Helen Keller, I can detach from all vision of what I expect to be shown by my experiences and I truly begin to See.

This point in time, in history, in mankind, we are witnessing an amazing global shift of consciousness. Look up. Look around. Look deeply. Then close your eyes and go.

There is no fear on this journey. I can sense angels rising up at my darkest moments, and I'm reminded of that moment on the road years ago. I am reminded of the sun's prostration across a cold winter's road, and then I know I am unbounded. And since all living things are connected, I know that, ultimately, we are all free.

So, ask yourself deep questions, look deeply at your life, look outside your life to all that this world is, and then come back to that big question, "Why am I here?"

Surrender to a Dream

Sri Swami Satchidananda said, "If you totally surrender yourself into the hands of God, you will feel, 'God, I didn't plan to come here. You sent me here. You have a purpose. I don't know what that purpose is. . . . let me always remember that you are working through me. I am not responsible for any of these things. Please let me not forget this.'"

Certainly this is not to say we are meant to lie around doing nothing, but rather that our doing is a surrendered allowing. Surrender is allowing. Allowing is surrender. We put up many blocks in our lives out of fear, only to bemoan why our lives aren't more fulfilling. This is where most of us get stuck.

What motivates you? What blocks you? What would your life look like if you allowed yourself to surrender to the great Unknown?

Time and again, I have made leaps of faith. I have met with painful losses and hard lessons, but did not let myself be defeated. For when you begin to offer your life up to the Greater Good, the hardest lessons sometimes arise. It is as if God is saying, "Oh, so you think you are ready to surrender to the Will of God or the Universe or Spirit?" The tests are to see your level of commitment, the power of your devotion. Embrace the trials and celebrate the lessons you learn, as this is how we truly grow.

I have surrendered again and again, swallowed pride and grown in understanding of the process. I refuse to allow myself to doubt or fear the outcome of my aspirations. I am allowing the Universe to work its magic through me. The more I say "I can," I can. The more I surrender, the more I see opening up. The more I allow, the more I see revealed.

Questions

Why are we here?
What are we doing?

Why are there so many people who are reaching towards Spirit and yet, finding they can't quite grasp the Light? Women especially seem to be caught in this modern day "gotta do" mode that has us running on empty, and no amount of time on the cushion or mat seems to lift the weight bearing down upon us long enough to feel a sense of rejuvenation.

Living in the Light – Living for Service – Living with Purpose

For me, that's all there is, and that is all I am here to do. Yet, it is critical to be supported and guided and self-sustained through this journey.

I reach out to students of all ages through Yoga, to clients through astrology or *Feng Shui*, and I see the benefits of serving and offering Light in various ways to many people who (just like me) are seeking.

Seeking a sense of peace.
Seeking a sense of "I am okay" and "my life is enough."
Seeking a sense that they are loved and supported.
Seeking.

Why are you here?
What are you doing?

Climbing the Jewel Tree

As children on a spiritual path we first stand at the roots of the Jewel Tree. We look up in wonder, and that is the moment of realization. We suddenly see beyond our limited reality. We begin to climb and discover the first easily accessible branches. These are the first Teachers we encounter who awaken us to the Unknown—friends, family, a minister or rabbi, an author, a political figure, a school teacher, or a Yoga instructor. We play on these branches with the innocence of the Fool.

Some of us so enjoy this place that we contentedly remain here for the rest of our lives. Others continue to seek, wonder, question, and explore. As we open ourselves to the answers, new Teachers arrive. Perhaps discovered through a recommended book, a lecture a friend took us to, or maybe a major event that profoundly propels us forward, as if leaping into the arms of an unknown figure who we inherently know to trust.

So we climb more branches of the Jewel Tree, and here we discover monks, clergy, and other devout religious figures. We study their teachings, we take up ritual, and we take up practices such as chanting, meditation, prayer, or joining a *sangha*. After a while, we've gone through the same process again, but now it seems easier to look, easier to deepen our inquiry to Know. Seeing all the shimmering jewels around us—so much wisdom, so much joy, so much love and peace—uplifting our hearts, our souls thirst for Enlightenment.

This time we Know that there is no need to continue climbing, for the rest of the tree will open up to us by our simply being still and allowing. Expanding this View we discover the intense Light of Buddhas, Bodhisattvas, and other Enlightened Masters. We welcome them into our practice, into our souls, into our lives.

Resting now in the heart of the Jewel Tree, we can surrender to the *dharma* supported by our initial teachers, inspired by our current growing practice and *sangha*, and uplifted by the Light and the truths of all those Enlightened Ones.

No wind, no storm, no act of man or beast can sway you from your perch. This is the place where the Spiritual Journey ends and the Path truly begins.

Purposeful Living

As a cloud, the cloud does not become consumed with fear when it is time to rain. Feeling itself fill with moisture, the cloud recognizes its purpose to nourish the Earth and many living beings. If the cloud were to hold the rain in fear, thinking, "Oh, no, I'm afraid of letting go. I want to hold this for myself. I'm afraid of what will happen when I let go." Then much suffering would ensue. But if the cloud trusts its purpose and itself enough, then when it fills with moisture, it knows immediately what to do—it lets go and lets the moisture fall as rain. The cloud would then feel great joy in seeing all the benefits that action has upon so many living things.

Trusting in your purpose here in this life, in this now moment, is the key to feeling true contentment. Knowing that your purpose is one that brings benefit, positive influence, and maybe even joy to others, is the greatest paycheck you could ever bank on.

As a tree, the tree does not cling to every leaf it unfurls in spring. The leaves and the tree nourish each other through the seasons of spring and summer, caring for each other unconditionally. The tree does not say to the leaves, "If you don't transform the sunshine into nutrients for me to grow I will take you from my branch!" Nor do the leaves retaliate against the tree by saying, "If you don't give us what we want then we will fall to the ground and leave you bare." No, both the tree and the leaves give openly to each other without condition. So, when the leaves change in the autumn, both the leaves and tree recognize that the time has come to separate. The purpose of their relationship has ended and transforms. As the leaves fall the tree does not try to cling to them and the leaves do not try to hang on to the branch. They have cared for each other with nonattachment, unconditionally and with devotion. The leaves that have fallen lie at the foot of the tree through the winter decomposing and becoming compost to nourish the roots of the tree. Even though they are separate from each other they continue to have a symbiotic relationship.

So, recognize that your purpose today may be different tomorrow. Like the bamboo, we must bend to these changes without clinging, without resistance, and without resentment. Accept that each day you have a purpose that is determined by the needs of those around you, whether it is at work, at school, at home, or in your community.

Remember, your purpose is to offer yourself in service from a place of inner peace and know that cultivating your truest Self comes only through the practice of meditation. The daily practice of sitting silent and still, aware of your breath, is as essential as drinking clean water or getting a good night's sleep.

The purposeful life is one in which we do not look for reward, recognition or any sort of acknowledgement for our actions—we offer our service freely, unconditionally, and joyfully. Even if your family, your work or your community is not ideally how you would like it to be, you still hold fast to your purpose and to sharing your inner peace, your true Self, as needed, in whatever capacity, to the best of your ability.

Adjust, Adapt, and Accommodate

The hard ground of winter does not resist warming to spring, softening itself to allow infinite numbers of plants and trees to manifest from its fertile soil. The caterpillar does not enter the chrysalis kicking and screaming, "I refuse to become anything other than what I am!" What is life but change, an endless cycle of experience? Life is learning, growing, sickness, healing, being born, and dying.

Yoga is a path upon which we learn to accept change with greater grace and ease. It is far more pleasant to bend like the bamboo to the winds of change, conflict and obstruction, than to hold yourself rigid with resistance, refusal and despair. The very asanas of Hatha Yoga are just that—bending with ease and grace. To resist would cause injury or ineffectiveness.

Our world is constantly presenting us with something new to adapt to, whether it's the weather, the price of gas, or your job. I've counseled many people regarding their professional path when they've become unemployed. Over and over again I find that people would rather continue to knock on the familiar door of what they know than to turn around and find a new door to try.

Sri Swami Satchidananda says, ". . . if you are able to adjust, adapt, and accommodate, you are able to rise above those situations. Do your daily work, deal with everyone, move with everybody. Be the ocean, but learn to surf well."

When a situation arises:

- **Adjust** to the needs of the moment, whether that means adjusting your attitude, your position, or your view.

- **Adapt** to what is happening so as to maintain your inner peace, while allowing yourself to shift to allow for the best possible outcome.

- **Accommodate** the person, the situation, or condition with an open heart and mind with trust and faith that the outcome will be exactly what it is meant to be.

This is the AAA plan of Yoga, it is a great insurance policy to support your well-being through the cycles and changes of life.

A three-year-old named May sat down between two classmates where there wasn't enough room. Still, she pushed and squeezed her way in, complaining the whole time, "I need more room! Miss Nitya, they won't let me sit here!" Of course, there is no reasoning with a three-year-old, but I did ask her to move back where there was plenty of space, to which she firmly resisted. Meanwhile, the other two kids were discomforted and disturbed by the intrusion and were not willing to accommodate this child forcing her way in. May was steadfast on sitting exactly where she wanted to sit, as were the other two children. Not one was willing to make change to solve the issue, so all three were miserable. It was a perfect example for what happens in our lives when we do not adjust, adapt, and accommodate.

We are just fine until something or someone comes along and jams their views, their influence, or their presence into our peaceful space. We can adjust, adapt and accommodate to make it far easier and more pleasant or escalate to a fight of resistance. In the end, when you adopt the Yoga AAA insurance policy, who wins? We all win! It has nothing to do with getting what we want, it is about acceptance, it is about allowing, it is about compromise, and it is about open-hearted/open-minded compassion.

A Time of Change

So we have come to this place, a place where we are being forced into change. As much as we want to resist and cling to old ways, old modes of behavior and relating, they no longer fit with the paradigm that we are in now.

Look at your relationships. Do they have the depth that your soul craves? Are you experiencing meaningful interaction with your friends, your partner, and your children? Are you really connecting with them? And if not, how do you release whatever is holding you back? Is it time to shift *who* you are relating to, or is it just a matter of shifting yourself? Is it that you need to delve deeper and open that well-spring of love within yourself? Do you need to nurture and love your own self so you will naturally attract the relationships that are meant to be in your life? And is it time to look deeply at those with whom you're negatively entangled? Why do they linger? How do you free yourself from them peacefully, lovingly, with compassion, and forgiveness? How do you stop battling and let go?

What is so terrifying about letting go? What would happen? Is it that you can't imagine that you are that good, that you are that deserving, or that you are that capable of having loving, meaningful relationships in your life? And yet we all at some point in our lives are faced with taking that leap.

One by one you see people around you taking that leap, breaking free of relationships that no longer serve them, moving past friendships that no longer seem to resonate, exploring their talents, seeking out more meaningful work. What happens when you allow yourself to be your Authentic Self? When you break free from the fear and concern that you will be rejected, thought a freak, strange, rebellious, for simply standing out and saying, "This is my great I Am. This is who I am, and I am filled with love for this Self. And I welcome you into this circle if you are ready to relate to me from this place of authenticity."

Maybe we need to gather in more circles—circles of women, circles of men, circles of children, circles of families—and truly look at each other as our own mirror, our own reflection, to let healing begin, forgiveness begin, growth begin, meaningful living begin from this place of living our Authentic Selves. Free from the entrapments of tradition, status quo, and what's popular, you are just standing out in your own Light saying, "Yes, this is my great I AM."

But first you have to ask yourself what is that—who is that? How do you find out if you haven't tapped into that depth of Self? How? How do you discover your True Self? Journaling your thoughts, meditation, and Hatha Yoga everyday—not as a chore, not as something you have to do, but something that nourishes your soul—opens you into your Heart Space and connects you to your Authentic Self, so that you can fall in Love with that beautiful Spirit, bask in that Light, and shine it out to the world.

The Answers

. . . have patience with everything unresolved in your heart
and try to love the questions themselves . . .
Don't search for the answers,
which could not be given to you now,
because you would not be able to live them.
And the point is to live everything.
Live the questions now.
Perhaps then, someday far in the future,
you will gradually, without even noticing it,
live your way into the answer.

—RAINER MARIA RILKE

We are conditioned to strive, to push, and to sweat it out as we attempt to achieve goals in life. But the Universe does not work on a schedule, knows no calendar, and tends to not respond well to pushing through much of anything except maybe birthing a baby. As I wrote in an earlier Musing, about in-between times and accepting difference in our lives, there is also a very important component of allowing, adjusting, adapting, surrendering. When I look back on my hardest lessons learned, often thought failures or mistakes at first—but I know there are no failures and no mistakes—what I find is that I pushed too hard, I forced something to happen, and the end result was not successful. It's not to say that we should not strive for goals, like working hard for a degree or applying for a job, or tilling a plot of land. It's when we are lost, when we don't have the answers, but are plagued with questions, when obstacles arise that seem insurmountable, that it is best to take a step back. And in looking at a situation that is stuck, or you don't have a direction in which to go, you surrender.

One spring I found myself lost and floundering without direction. I knew there was no point in struggling through the fog that seemed impenetrable around me, and so I focused on what was working, what was flowing, and had to accept that some answers simply weren't ready for me to know yet. That is a big dose of patience pudding, my friends! And my Yoga practice, my Buddhist faith, and the guidance from the *I Ching* were instrumental in keeping me grounded, calm, and focused on the road ahead, even if I couldn't see the road.

And what evolved, what blossomed as a result of that surrendering, was like the clouds in my sky finally lifted to reveal a bright shining sun. It wasn't that I was searching, I was simply open, when a great gift from the Universe, a clear, new path filled with love, revealed itself. That was the energy needed to move forward into a new place, literally.

This, I think to myself, is the magic of living a life that is accepting of the questions, recognizing that often the answers cannot always be immediately known. We should always trust that the Universe provides exactly what is needed for the journey we are ultimately to live. The answers come if we are willing to listen long enough with our hearts open. The answers do come.

Change: The In-Between Times

It's hard to get used to different.

Change can be a sudden thing, like a car crash, death of a loved one, graduation, vacation, etc. Other times change is a slow, evolving, organic process that moves you from one place or relationship or state of being to the next. Awareness of your Self and your life's journey at least alerts you to the subtle shifts as you process change. Change can be scary. Change can cause stress. Change can affect many aspects of your life. There is an awkwardness to change: as you move from one place to the next you experience a time of in-between. It is this time of in-between when we feel the most ungrounded—you're not in the job or out of a job, you're not in a relationship or out of a relationship, you're just floating in-between, not feeling grounded in one thing or the other, just floating. It's the floating, the ungroundedness that often makes people the most stressed out about change, about being stuck in the in-between, because only the Universe really knows what that next thing is. You can apply for 100 jobs and want desperately any one of them, but only the Universe can say any of those jobs was meant to be yours.

So in change there is an element of surrender; in Yoga we call this *Ishvara Pranidhana*. And with surrender comes an enormous amount of faith and trust that a higher power is there, guiding you in your life. Even if you don't have a compass, even if you're in a time where you can't find true north, you can surrender to the great Divine, knowing wherever you wind up, wherever and with whom, that you will be okay.

It's like the ages from 11–15, when you're neither child nor adult, and you feel torn between one and the other. Part of you still feels like a kid and part of you really wants to be grown, but being an adult is kind of scary with so much responsibility. Resisting change seems normal because we've all been a teenager, but we also rebel as adults too. We complain about where we are, but as soon as we have something new, we complain about how different it is from what we had. Are we ever satisfied?

September is back-to-school time, a harbinger of change and the end of summer. I remember being a kid realizing summer vacation was coming to a close as those last weeks of August melted away in the haze of sweltering hot days. The anxiety would slowly build up as that first day of school approached. The shift towards going back to school was the ultimate in-between time for me. I can still feel it, because even now my own schedule changes and a totally different day-to-day life unfolds come September.

We must learn to surrender with faith in the in-between times and embrace different. The alternative is to be stressed and anxious, which will only lead to wrong turns. Instead recognize that the road ahead is not always visible through the fog of the great Unknown, but trust that it will reveal itself when the time is right. The Universe doesn't work by a calendar or any set schedule. The Universe works in an organic, karmic flow of energy.

It's time to hit the ocean of our lives, my friends. It's time to surf into different.

It's Not the Size of the Flower Pot . . .
Well, Maybe It Is.

For all that I constantly have to do, I am sure you are just as busy managing all the aspects of your life and the roles you play from day to day. There are times when I am tempted to learn another skill or trade, to venture into another big project, and then I stop as I see how full my life already is and I say, "no thank you."

My life can be compared to a flower pot, containing one flower. It has many petals, and each makes up some part of who I am—the roles I play, all that I am committed to and responsible for. Some petals are unnamed and unclaimed, left to be the empty spaces in my life where I might find a morning or a whole day to do and be nothing or anything.

When you buy your spring plantings they often come in small black plastic containers. When you pull the plant out to put in the ground, you see how the roots are all bound up and compressed in the shape of the container. How well would this plant have flourished if it never had the opportunity to exist in a larger environment? It can be scary going from the familiar, small coziness of what we know into the realm of the Unknown, just like that plant; but look at all we'd miss learning and experiencing.

So it was that after many years living in a little house on Maple Avenue, I woke up one day, mid-winter, and thought just this thought. I realized I felt stifled, restricted, and started to entertain the idea of more space. Ultimately, despite the efforts of helpful friends and much time driving around Richmond, a house found me. Moving to a larger house in a quieter neighborhood gave everyone, including my dog, more space to live and grow. Replanted in this new home, I hoped our roots would stretch and spread with renewed possibilities and blessings. In fact, within the first week of living there my business began to flourish. Within myself I felt a great exhalation. I wonder if a plant from a tiny pot, moving into a larger pot, responds in the same way?

Have you jammed too much into your flower pot? Are there weeds crowding your roots? Is it time for another pot? It's an analogy worth contemplating.

Musings on Renewing

It is the most *yin* of all the seasons—darker, colder, quieter. Winter is the perfect opportunity to find time to freeze your date book and silence your cell phone. It's the time to allow yourself to be still and silent. I say this over and over again to my students—allow yourself to be still and silent.

I challenge you to create a weekend this January (or any time) when you can curl into your home for a Silent Retreat. If you have family, then arrange for them to go on an adventure of their own, so everyone benefits. Go into, say, three days with no agenda or expectations. Begin by purging your body of toxins with a one-day fast. Sri Swami Satchidananda says in his book *To Know Yourself*, "In normal daily life it's good to fast one day a week, taking only water or fruit juices—no dairy products. During the other days be careful in eating: don't overload your system. You will always feel light and be healthy."

Fast on the first day, and during this day you can do some gentle, slow Hatha, meditation, and journaling. Journaling is a wonderful way to purge the mind of your thoughts, ideas, dreams, problems and worries. For day two you can eat a little something mid-day, like plain yogurt with honey, while still drinking lots of water. Yogi Teas makes a Detox blend that helps the body release toxins. Your tongue will tell you, because it will coat over. (A complete detox fast can take several days and is complete when the tongue returns to its natural pink color and saliva becomes sweet.) If you do a more extensive fast, consult a professional for guidance. Then, as day two progresses, have a light dinner, such as brown rice and steamed veggies—a modest portion. On day three have a light breakfast, like oatmeal with yogurt and dried fruits, a lunch of salad, and finally at dinner eat something like lentils, brown rice, and steamed dark greens.

Aside from diet to cleanse the body, you are also working on cleansing through daily Hatha and meditation. Of course one of the more decadently delicious aspects of a home Silent Retreat is sleeping later and napping, which help your body refuel and repair. Just let the rest of the world melt away for these days of freedom from electronics or outside contact. To truly go within you must not give yourself opportunities for distraction. *Mauna* means silence in Sanskrit. Bring that space within you—guide it, and in-lighten it with the sacred sound of OM and awaken anew!

Stepping into Your Own Light

The obstacle to your own success in life is fear. The ego constantly loops a recording of self-doubt, questioning, worry and self-criticism in our minds, paralyzing us from truly living our lives fully. The question remains: "What would you do, who would you be, if you disengaged from that ego voice in your head and stepped into Your Own Light?" Your Light is your true potential, a space where solutions come from an awareness of yourself, requiring no effort, just allowing.

Many years ago I began to learn and work with the teachings of Geshe Tenzin Wangal Rinpoche on creating inner stillness, silence, and spaciousness. My career skyrocketed as a result of that practice. Projects I didn't think I could accomplish all came together synchronistically. I opened the space, with no attachment to the outcome, and allowed the work to manifest spontaneously on its own. All the right people presented themselves; I never had to doubt a single one involved, they all came because they were attracted to the space and the work that was being done.

Most important of all is to cultivate an "open heart." *Bhakti* Yoga, the Yoga of Devotion, is the path that reminds us that nothing in life is fulfilling, successful or rewarding, without a heart full of gratitude, compassion, and love. When your heart is open, the space that is created around you should be fully trusted. Your Love is the strongest, most powerful force inside you—this is the Light that you long to step into. This Light, this Love, is indestructible. Nothing and no one can destroy it. You become your own superhero. Surrendered into that space, you can truly accomplish anything. What I have accomplished in my own work truly amazes me, humbles me, and confirms the power of the path I am on to affect positive change in the world.

I have stepped into my own Light, and I am not alone—I have never been so supported. I have no idea where this will take me, what will happen next, but I neither question nor doubt it—I simply open up inside, abiding in the space of my heart, and follow that Light. We must be courageous with ourselves, trust our potential, and open our hearts fully to loving ourselves for exactly who we are at this now moment in our lives. From this space, abide quietly, be still with your thoughts, and the Light will spark in you a whole new paradigm of being.

Meditate by stilling the body—you don't have to be so busy, do so much. Just be. Meditate on stilling the mind. Let the stream of thoughts run by without engaging; eventually they will slow down. Over time, with a dedicated practice, distracting thoughts will subside. Meditate on creating spaciousness and openness in your heart. Breathe into the space of the heart with loving-kindness, an unconditional love that accepts *who* you are, just *as* you are. Through meditating on stillness, silence, and spaciousness, your life will open up, and you will find it to be a very natural moment when you are STANDING IN YOUR OWN LIGHT, Self-realized, more fully alive, present and joyful than you ever thought possible.

E Ma Ho!
How Wonderful!

Getting Unstuck

We all experience times when we get mired down. Think of a time when you were aimlessly moving through the days, as if you were walking through mud with your head in the clouds. You couldn't move fast, and you were overlooking so many obvious things.

Here's one such experience I had. I spent weeks intending to vacuum the house, only to meet with one good excuse after another: "It's raining, and mud and leaves are being tracked in, so the house will just get dirty again—might as well wait"; or "My back aches, and I'm just not up to doing it today." I did eventually sweep the hardwood floors, but I just couldn't get myself to open the closet door and haul that bad boy out to get the job done. The block within me to do this simple task was immense!

Finally, I did it—opened the closet door, hauled said vacuum out. Doing so prompted the thought, "When did I last check the bag?" Sure enough—the bag was stuffed, and I had no replacements. I laughed right out loud at the irony. Needless to say, it took another week to buy the bags from the vacuum store down the street. It took another week before I put a bag in the machine. Then came the day of victory, when it took all of 30 minutes to run the vacuum through my house, even stopping to clean the moldings and cobwebs. I felt relieved. The silly block had finally been lifted.

How do we let ourselves get to these places anyway? Is it simply that our "bag" is too full to do the job? Perhaps we should take the lesson here to check in every so often to see if we're getting "full." Are we, in fact, pushing our internal machine too far, too hard, for too long? If I had vacuumed without first checking the bag, the house would not have gotten clean, the dirt would have just been pushed around with only some of it getting sucked up. Point being: we can only do our work well when we have the capacity to put our full energies towards the task.

What happens to the human body when it is put under stress, duress, conflict, or tension for long periods of time without a break? What happens when an overloaded vacuum cleaner is used over and over despite the bag being full? It works poorly, and then the motor could burn out. We have to properly maintain and care for ourselves—to empty that proverbial bag of energy—and properly clean our "house."

Slowing Down to Heal

Continuing with the analogy of the vacuum cleaner . . .

Again. What happens to the human body when it is put under stress for long periods of time without a break? What happens when an overloaded vacuum cleaner is used over and over despite the bag being full? It stops working well and could eventually blow up.

When you have pushed your life to the limit with predicaments like financial calamity, failing business, issues at work, a really taxing schedule, relationship troubles or divorce, or maybe a terminally-ill loved one, it takes a toll on all levels—physical, mental, and spiritual. If these problems persist, it is most certainly the case of a very full vacuum cleaner bag. I guarantee you are not functioning at peak capacity. In fact, you are probably pushing yourself as hard as you can just to survive each day.

My story begins when I shuttered my Yoga studio in late spring of 2008, drove to Long Island for my brother's wedding weekend, and spent a month getting the bankruptcy processed. After all of this I thought my troubles were behind me. And for the most part they were, but what I never imagined was that the stress from the past three years, of raising a special needs child while running a studio, only to see the studio crumble, was deeply residing in my cellular body.

In fact, that year of my life after the bankruptcy took a far slower, more easeful pace, yet I was getting sicker and sicker. I couldn't understand why I was so tired when I was doing so much less? Why could I not focus or keep my mind clear? How had I lost all ambition to move forward? Why was I hungry right after I'd eaten, like I couldn't get enough? Then my back started to lock up, affecting my Hatha Yoga practice. By early August of that year I woke up in so much pain, radiating from my lower back into my hip and knee joints, that it was all I could do to get out of bed to take pain medicine.

I knew something was terribly wrong. I put in a "911 call" to my friend for acupuncture, and later that week another friend spent hours giving me craniosacral massage. I felt a degree of relief. I also began to see that I needed to release some stuff, but what? I couldn't imagine what I was holding onto. I thought maybe this was a sacroiliac issue and I needed a chiropractic adjustment. I figured, with the battery of symptoms I had, I needed someone who could treat me with an arsenal of cures, so I called a naturopath. The saliva tests and other tests we took that initial day revealed adrenal dysfunction. I knew about adrenal glands from Yoga anatomy training, and knew a few poses that benefited these little glands that sit on top of the kidneys. But what do the adrenals do?

The adrenals' primary job is to help your body manage stress, but if your life is immersed in stress and the adrenals can no longer function well (think clogged vacuum), that is where the trouble begins. I would imagine millions of Americans are suffering from a certain amount of adrenal stress disorder because of our relentless lifestyle.

Some of the symptoms, besides the ones I mentioned, are: digestive trouble, anxiety attacks, moodiness, headaches, menstrual irregularity, mental fogginess, back pain, joint pain, fatigue, shakiness, and more. Many doctors misdiagnose and treat this disorder with antidepressants. Untreated adrenal dysfunction can lead to Addison's disease, where the adrenals simply shut down, but this is pretty rare.

The eye-opener for me was when the naturopath said that *Yoga had helped to save my life*. Wow! I made modifications to my diet. I began to sleep more and take naps during the day. In the beginning I slept upwards of 16 hours a day! I had to let go of the guilt of not being so productive and surrender to this time of healing. I also took a lot of herbal supplements to help support my adrenals and my body's return to balance. After several weeks I was able to get out of bed in the morning with ease, I slept through the night, I could run a little with my dog, and I was back to my Yoga practice with far more flexibility.

I found that time to be a huge wake up call. I felt I owed my body an apology for pushing it so hard for so long. We were healing together.

Alternative healing practices like acupuncture, chiropractic adjustments, craniosacral massage, and working with a naturopath offer greater opportunities for healing the body and targeting the cause than passive pill popping. Just like that vacuum cleaner with the full bag, if you just looked at the symptoms, you'd have thought the vacuum was broken and needed to be replaced. You have to open it up, look inside, and determine the real cause of the problem—it needed a fresh bag.

I share this intimate story with you because I want to illuminate the importance of balance in your own life. The need to ease up on your schedule, or at the least take time every day to take a nap, meditate, and be still and silent. Yoga, my friends, is a critical tool in allowing your body to heal itself and to better manage the stress in your life.

Heal Yourself

In this world of therapeutic options—advanced medicine, alternative healing services, and weight loss gurus—is it possible to heal ourselves?

Let's say that it is possible. Know then that you are the root from which all of your life has germinated, budded, bloomed, and has the ability to further manifest. Most medicines, when they work, do not work by directly fixing what's wrong inside you, but by influencing your body's systems to correct themselves. *You* heal you. So what things can you do to unlock your potential to move from *dis*-ease to ease?

Let's start from the top—look at your state of mind. A mind that is clear, accepting, adapting, and open to life's possibilities is one of positive potency. A mind full of wonder, hope, gratitude, and compassion has less conflict and greater potential. *Dis*-ease begins when that attitude turns negative, whether directed towards yourself or someone else. Over time, a chronic negative message will take up residency within the body. Depression, panic, hatred, all waste precious energy and kill our potential. Grief that has not been processed effectively can turn into fibromyalgia, chronic lung ailments, and arthritis or stiff joints. Repressed anger can flare up into a cancer. Heart disease can often be linked to issues with love and relationships. Chronic negativity is one of the main causes of disease, born of the stress you are putting on the body.

Beyond your attitude there is what you are eating and drinking. So much illness can stem from an unhappy digestive system. Are you consuming enough water every day? A great book to read is *Your Body's Many Cries for Water: You are Not Sick, You are Thirsty* by Fereydoon Batmanghelidj. We're water beings—we need *water*. Likewise, if you want to get the most use out of a car, you have to put not only enough fuel in it, but the *right kind* of fuel. The human body's design was completed eons before most modern food ingredients were developed, and they really don't belong in the system. I'm of the opinion that more than half of the food in grocery stores should not be eaten. Processed foods, frozen dinners, soft drinks, and nearly everything down that cracker/cookie/cereal aisle has nothing to offer your body in the way of good health. It is dead energy.

If you find cooking simple, wholesome meals an overwhelming task requiring too much time, thought, and money, you are cheating yourself and your family of vibrant well-being. Eating well costs less because it keeps you and your loved ones healthier. In fact, the digestive system itself is the epicenter from which our body experiences wellness or illness. So if you're unwell, look first at your diet before reaching for a bottle of pills. If you find your children are regularly on antibiotics and struggling with allergies, you definitely want to consult with a nutritionist. I wrote *The Yoga with Nitya Cookbook: Seasonal, Local, Vegetarian Meals for a Healthy Family* expressly to ease the conundrum of how to cook great meals by making it far simpler and easier to manage.

An optimum diet consists of organic fruits and vegetables, whole grains, nuts and seeds, legumes, beans, local plain yogurt, milks made from almonds, coconuts or rice. Limit refined foods as much as possible and *avoid GMO entirely*—read labels!

Next, you need to look at how you are moving your body. We live in a very sedentary world where we sit at desks, in cars, and on the couch more than ever before. Regular exercise is so important, not just for the movement itself, but for the fact that moving the body increases the body's ability to build bone and muscle, absorb nutrition, digest effectively, and eliminate the toxins from the body as well. Other benefits include a calmer mind and more rejuvenating sleep.

Explore all kinds of exercises, whether it be Yoga, Pilates, *Chi Gong*, biking, swimming, walking, or running. These types of activities can be done weekly, but really you want to do something that motivates you to get up. Yep, *get up!* Start with just 15 minutes of movement. I know from experience Hatha Yoga is great for invigorating the metabolism, digestion, and is an overall tonic for functions of all systems of the body. The great thing about Hatha Yoga is that anyone can do it, even at home, even in a chair.

I know you brush your teeth at least once a day, so why not "brush your mind?" Meditation will all but guarantee a better night's sleep and a more easeful day. Meditation practiced in the morning and at night returns your mind to its natural state of calm and quiet. Learning to sit still and silently with yourself is of vital importance to your well-being.

When emotions get stuck and stress intensifies, journaling your thoughts can be a creative and powerful release. Often, looking at your issues on a page helps you see them in a new light. I encourage everyone to journal at least once a week not just to free their minds of the events of the day but to build a loving, compassionate relationship with Self.

You have the ability, wisdom, and choice to heal yourself, starting this very moment. This advice is to encourage you to prevent illness from taking root, and to reverse it every way you can. Applying these self-healing principles while under a doctor's care for an existing condition will boost your immune system, and quicken your recovery.

Stop and look deeply at how you take care of yourself—body, spirit, and mind.

So, can you heal yourself?

Yes, you can.

Finding Balance

It is not enough to be busy. . . .
The question is:
What are we busy about?

—THOREAU

So, are you busy? Undoubtedly most of us can say, with a twinge of annoyance in our voices, a resounding "YES" to that question. Yet, despite our fatigue and our feeling overwhelmed during our day, that question persists, "What are you busy about?"

Was that not *you* that said yes to all that you are doing? Or have you allowed yourself to be volunteered to do some, and maybe hired to do some, and maybe felt a sense of duty to do some. . . . All of that sums up to *too much*. The scale of your time and energy has swung far out of balance.

I came home one day, needing to work at my desk, but wound up doing dishes, picking up around the house, doing laundry, and walking the dogs. By the time I sat down I went from having three hours to having just one hour to do the work. I wondered how people manage all of their workload when they work outside of the home. Do people come home to dishes in the sink, clothes in the dryer, rooms needing to be straightened after a full day in the office? I can see how quickly the stack of things needing to be done could become staggering and push someone over the edge into overwhelm. I am grateful to at least have some flexibility in my day to manage all that I've volunteered for, been hired to do, and that I feel responsible for. Some days I struggle to find balance and to feel a sense of both harmony and accomplishment.

In the midst of your day you ride waves of energy. If you are present, then you are aware of the flow of your day. In any given moment you can choose to put down your phone, gaze out a window and just breathe. In any given moment you can choose to say "no" to a task when you know your schedule is full. In any given moment you can choose how you use your time. Despite what it may look like, we really do have more options and more control over our lives than we think. Look at your daily calendar and ensure every day you have allotted time to be still and alone with yourself, even if for just 15 minutes. Schedule "me time" to gain ease and shed stress.

Eknath Easwaran says:

"We need time simply to be quiet now and then: time to reflect on what we are doing, what we value, how we are spending our lives. Living in balance means living in the present, ready for whatever comes. When your life is in balance, you lose the capacity to be disappointed."

Finding Comfort within the Discomfort

A swami once told me that Hatha Yoga is not intended to be comfortable, but rather, the goal or focus is to "find the comfort within the discomfort." I found that statement to be profound wisdom—so much so that I've adopted it into the catalog of mantras I live by.

As I shared this juicy bit of wisdom in a Yin class, I could see that truth playing out as we held our poses for five minutes, breathing through the discomfort, adapting to the discomfort, sinking into the discomfort, finding a way to abide in the discomfort until the gong chimed. Then the counter-pose allowed us all to release the tension and snuggle into comfort with a slightly easier breath. It is such a powerful lesson in not only our Hatha Yoga practice, but how we manage ourselves on any given day.

Life itself is not designed to be comfortable. I think this is true throughout the animal kingdom. What we do daily, from the moment we wake up, is wiggle, struggle, and work our way from one interaction to the next situation looking for comfort. We seek comfort through food, clothing, our home, our chair, our car, our shower, our recreation, our sleep, our work environment, our relationships, our own skin.

And is our finding peace not tied interdependently with being comfortable? Yet we squirm on our meditation cushions with occasional adjustments, feeling the ache in our knees, the weariness of our spines to keep us erect, and our busy monkey-minds swinging on the vines of random thoughts. . . . Where is the comfort? Where is the peace?

So within weeks of embracing this mantra I was greatly tested and challenged by the concept. I awoke one morning with terrible muscle pain and cramping in my back that I attributed to sitting poorly for long stretches at my desk. Days passed and the pain eased some but manifested anew in my abdomen. I blamed that affliction on gluten, thinking that my dinner at a restaurant was the culprit. But many days later, I struggled terribly with pain in my digestive system with increasing worry as to exactly what the root of this pain was.

I finally resolved to go to the emergency room. So all of these issues were actually appendicitis! As I lay in my hospital bed that night, recovering from surgery, I began to meditate on the mantra of finding comfort within extreme discomfort. For the weeks of healing I had to adjust myself and my life constantly, finding even my thinking and emotions to be uncomfortable. I wanted out of this body that had become so foreign to me. A fundamental Yoga *sutra* is: "What you focus on expands." I found my strength through focusing on any glimmer of comfort I could find. Just like being immersed in a deep darkness, eventually a spark of light can be found and by focusing on it—it expands.

Comfort can be found within discomfort when we apply patience, mindful breathing, and the evolved wisdom that everything is temporary, everything is in constant change and flux. For most of us, a good portion of our day is relatively comfortable, especially when we look at those who are suffering terrible atrocities—locally, nationally, and worldwide.

The end product of finding comfort within the discomfort is this: gratitude. For every moment that I am present and aware of being comfortable, I am supremely grateful. But I am also grateful for the discomforts that are there as a teaching tool, to gain greater perspective, to expand and grow from. I am profoundly grateful for all the help, prayers, and love given me by so many people as I recovered from the appendectomy. But even when we must suffer alone, gratitude is the thread that leads you from discomfort to comfort.

Five Ways to Stay Positive

I am grateful for the teachings of Yoga, which remind me I have the power to hold the Light within myself, even when the world around me feels cast in shadows. *Pratipaksha Bhavana* is the Yoga teaching on turning negatives into positives. It is known that people who are positive are generally healthier, live longer, have a better quality of life, and have more friends. So how do you stay positive in our world today?

1) **Avoid the news.** Seriously? Yes! Glance the headlines for truly relevant articles, but avoid the drama and always, always question the motive, the factuality, and the sources.

2) **Limit how much time you spend on social media.** Make a point to post positive images and words while avoiding getting sucked into everyone else's drama, along with the shared "news" stories designed to enrage and terrify you.

3) **Find that silver lining.** When you are thinking negative thoughts about yourself, others, or events happening, turn it around, be creative, and *just turn it around*. The good is there.

4) **Before you speak or act, ask yourself if you are spreading Light or dark in the world.** Turn your negative words and actions into positive ones. If that seems impossible in the moment, then be silent.

5) **Make a mental list of things you are grateful for.** Each day pause to do this and remain mindful of it. Even on the worst days there is *something* you can see as a blessing.

Be the Light

Did I offer peace today?
Did I bring a smile to someone's face?
Did I say words of healing?
Did I let go of my anger and resentment?
Did I forgive? Did I love?
These are the real questions.
I must trust that the little bit of love that I sow now
will bear many fruits, here in this world
And the life to come.

—HENRI NOUWEN

Violent words and actions are rooted in ignorance. This ignorance is all about attachments—attachments to belief systems, habits, the "need" for things to be a certain way. But life is ever-evolving and ever-changing. The malaise of a country or culture can be the result of pandemic ignorance manifested in an irrational desire that things stay the same or revert back to some wished-for, idealized past when things seemed better.

You know what makes life better? We do! You and me, friend! Come on, the dark negativity around us can only be lifted when we shine our Light of positivity, especially in the face of oppression, aggression, and conflict.

We cannot know what the future holds, but we can direct the course of our own lives, our own day-to-day by being the best we can be.

Live from your heart, be that brave, and shine brightly your Light.

The Day of the *Hotei*

On the day of a festival I decided I would only accept checks and credit cards. No cash. The week had been so busy I hadn't given much thought to revenue, but more to having all the products, flyers, and staffing needed for the event. At the last minute I decided to take my cash box, even though it was empty. As the day went on I sold lots of bumper stickers, incense, and other items, and each time I opened my cash box it was more full. I did not have a single credit card or check payment all day! By the time of the last sale, a customer handed me a $100 bill, and I said, "Somehow, I have change for that."

I realized at that moment that I had experienced the legend of the *Hotei*. You know, those happy, big-bellied statues from Asian restaurants? As the legend goes, a Buddhist monk went into a village with an empty sack and from his empty sack he threw coins out to the children.

OUT OF NOTHING COMES EVERYTHING.
OUT OF AN EMPTY SACK, PROSPERITY MANIFESTED.

The manifestation had nothing to do with my attachment to an outcome or to my desire for income, but rather it came purely from Source, from the offering of the Universal Way.

In being so busy, I hadn't had time to devote to worrying about money and anticipating sales. I had been simply focused on taking care of the day-to-day needs of running two businesses. It's as if I found myself receiving exactly what I needed without reaching out anxiously for it.

I didn't so much feel lucky, just *blessed*. Each of us has the capacity to manifest prosperity from our proverbial "empty sack." I have learned that much of what we earn in life has nothing to do with a regular paycheck, but with our purpose and intention.

What do you do and why do you do it? Can you be satisfied trusting that from your own empty sack all you truly need will become manifest? There is magic to our living.

That day for me seemed exquisitely magical.

Overload

Perhaps we are all fried—credit maxed, schedule overloaded, no time left to organize all you have to do—and you find yourself in a spin cycle of perpetual doing.

Where is the pause button, the reset button, the rewind button? How do we learn to stop ourselves and the cycle of doing long enough to rein it all in?

Do you wake up refreshed in the morning? Do you find yourself pushing yourself through the day with coffee and crappy snacks? At day's end are you numbing out in front of the TV or computer because you just don't know what else to do?

Maybe the answer is as easy as wiping an entire day clear of anything and taking a "U Day" to make a U-turn in your life. On your day off you look at your calendar, you look at your to-do list, and you reassess what has to happen and what is non-essential. You reprioritize what is most important in your life and learn to let the rest go. In doing this you will begin to open hours, maybe even days, when you have nothing to do but NOTHING—yes, nothing. Could you do that? Would you be able to devote time to yourself like that, to rejuvenate yourself?

I learned recently of a woman who spends one day a week in silence, and that includes no cell phone, TV or computer. She meditates, reads, journals, takes long walks, looks out her window, and really allows herself time to be alone with her Self. She claims it has restored her sense of well-being. Her family and friends know that this is her silent day and know not to call or text. Her community supports and respects her choice.

If nothing else, even if all you have free is a few minutes in your day, make them sacred for your Self as much you can. Even if it's as simple as sitting in your car with the windows down, taking deep breaths; or walking the dog or yourself around the block without your cell phone; or eating a meal silently.

All of these suggestions add up to this: honor your time, because, ultimately, your time is your life. Your well-being is a result of how you spend your time.

Spring Cleaning Your Diet

Farmer's markets are now open year-round in some cities. Why is this important to know? Why am I so impassioned about eating local food? It's all part of spring cleaning our diets.

Some key points about the American diet:

- It has become too cheap (and easy) to eat really bad stuff

- We have forgotten what food is and how to cook it

- We have also forgotten what grows when

- We have lost the awareness of where our food comes from

- We've allowed taste to determine what we eat, contributing to a burgeoning of snack foods to keep our digestive systems constantly churning.

If you haven't read *Omnivore's Dilemma* by Michael Pollan or seen the documentary *Food Inc.*, then consider yourself undereducated on a critical subject. Food as we know it is endangered. But we—you and I—have the power with our buying choices to save it. How? You simply don't buy the stuff that makes you unhealthy, or is out of season, or contains ingredients no one can pronounce.

Buy food that is in-season, organic, and locally grown by a farmer near you, and in doing so you will discover something really special about what you are eating. That special ingredient is *pride*, because it feels really good to sit down to a table with dishes predominantly sourced from local farmers who picked that food within the last couple days.

When you eat something that has been recently harvested, it has more nutrition, tastes better, supports that local farm, and is better for the environment (no transcontinental or intercontinental shipping). It's a win-win. Once I spring cleaned my family's diet many years ago, I never went back. Barbara Kingsolver's book *Animal, Vegetable, Miracle* was my final inspiration in adopting a seasonal, local diet. We are all the healthier for that change. It also inspired me to write *The Yoga with Nitya Cookbook: Seasonal, Local, Vegetarian Meals for a Healthy Family.*

Seasonal Eating

In the previous century we began to burn petroleum to transport food from around the world to our local supermarkets to offer us *everything*, all the time, regardless of the season. This is a convenience, but at a cost to our planet, our local economy, and—oh yeah—*our health*. Just look at the labels on the food in your cupboard and fridge: green peppers from Israel or avocados from Mexico equals a heck of a lot of gasoline and resources to make that batch of guacamole. Also, if foods have to spend weeks in boats and ports to get to our stores, then they weren't ripened naturally, and you can't really say they're fresh, either. In every climate and season, there are only certain foods available, and those should be your primary choices. So maybe those unavailable ones you buy occasionally, not weekly.

Learn what grows seasonally in your area. In the Mid-Atlantic region, winter is made up of dark leafy greens like kale, spinach, chard, and collards. There are carrots, potatoes both white and sweet, and onions. The only fruits are apples that have been stored from last autumn.

Spring brings asparagus in April, along with strawberries and those first salad greens. Let me tell you, I never buy store-bought strawberries anymore—they taste like plastic. A local, fresh-picked strawberry has the most *strawberriest* of flavor! Sadly, asparagus and strawberries are only around until early June.

As spring turns to summer there is a bounty of all kinds of berries, melons, peaches, greens, herbs, and too many veggies to name. As summer peaks it is canning and freezing time to ensure we have plenty of options for winter meals. I make dozens of jars of tomato sauce, salsa and canned peaches. I roast and freeze eggplant, peppers, tomatoes, zucchini and squash. Plus, I also make at least a dozen batches of pesto. Frozen fresh-picked blueberries are a delight to put in oatmeal or a cobbler.

As summer reaches late August the berries and peaches give way to apples and pears. Autumn arrives with tomatoes still available, broccoli, eggplant, peppers, leafy greens, and pumpkin (it's not just a decoration).

Once you get used to the seasonal foods in your area, you get into a rhythm with the earth that supports and sustains you the way Nature designed. By growing your own food, by shopping locally, by supporting your local farmers, you reduce your carbon footprint and do so much good for the local economy in addition to your overall well-being. Your meals will take on a whole new character and you'll feel pride in knowing that most of your meal was grown from local soil.

Let's get back to the table of our ancestors.

It ALL Matters

If realize any part of your day was dissatisfying, ask yourself why.

It ALL matters.

What we bring into our realm of consciousness is what our reality becomes. Look around at how we have created a separatist society fueled by an economic machine of more, more, more. And yet, are we happy with what we have? How much is enough? And while we're looking, let's not forget our neighbor, the homeless person on the street corner, the child starving across the border, or the nation at war across the ocean, because these are all our parts of our reality, born from this consciousness of greed and separation. We can't allow ourselves to go home and close the door each day, believing all that is undesirable is somewhere else.

It ALL matters.

While you are contemplating this, ask yourself what you did today to ease the suffering of another? How did you in-lighten our world today? If you have nothing to say to that, then your day is not done. You have work to do. The real work. The work that effects positive change.

It is scientifically proven that we are all connected. When significant events happen in the world, the ripples travel, and the energetic field of our global community feels it. This is like when you walk into a room after an argument has taken place—you can feel it.

It ALL matters.

When I teach Yoga to children, I teach them that we have the power to change the world with our own two hands. There are countless numbers of examples of people who span the globe, cultures, religions, and time, who made that difference by doing something that may have at first seemed small.

It all matters.

How we as a nation went from the horror of segregation in the first half of the twentieth century to an African-American President is the manifestation of collective, conscious change. This is our real work. If you believe we must eradicate hunger, do something about it. If you believe we should support local farmers, do something about. Every act you make every day is a vote for what you believe in. I believe in the power of love, and I teach this through Yoga, not always with words, not always with actions. Sometimes I walk into a room, sit down, close my eyes and simply embody love. I know that every person in that room benefits.

Do not disparage what others believe, just be open to understanding their view. I may see a sky as blue and you may see the sky as pink, but maybe my sky is at noon and yours is at dawn. How would I know if I don't try to understand but rather immediately argue or defend my view?

It all matters.

There is much to think about—upcoming elections, holidays, meetings, family events, and all the rest you have happening in your own life. I ask you again, to vote for what you believe in with your dollars, your vote, your words, your actions. We are all connected. How you vote is not just about you, it is about how that vote impacts your community, your nation, and our world.

It ALL matters.

I may never meet you, but I love you. All I can do is what I believe in. I am here to serve through love. What do you believe in? Why are you here? How do you make the world a better place with your own two hands?

It all matters.

—Inspired by the film *I AM*

Are You Drinking from the Well?

I had the extreme privilege of hearing my Yin Yoga teacher, Biff Mithoefer, speak at *satsang* in Yogaville. What he said *blew me away*. Sometimes it is just the right message at just the right time that really makes an unexpected impact. He spoke of recovering from the sudden loss of his wife, the well of grief he was lost in, and how he struggled to regain motivation to be in this world again.

I had always held to the idea that, in order to serve the world, I had to first serve myself—that by ensuring I was strong, well, and at peace, that I would be a better servant. He turned that notion on its head! Quoting Lao Tzu, he said: No, that it is by being of service, by easing the suffering of others, by lifting others up, that we in so doing ease our own suffering and are exalted. Then, after we have served, we come back to the Self, and we rest and nourish so that we can continue this work.

To truly serve, we need the spirit of Karma Yoga, the Yoga of selfless giving. Whether it is parenting your child, or in your romantic relationship, or in your job, or volunteering, how can you *truly* serve if your motivation is out of obligation, from an "I have to" mentality? Then you build up resentment that leads to suffering for all involved. By looking at the world as an extension of ourselves, we discover that our suffering is no different from anyone's, and that by touching another person's life with kindness and compassion, we too benefit.

It shouldn't take the holiday season for us to have food drives and other donations for the needy or community service. Get out and volunteer for the next election. Take an elderly neighbor something from your garden or something you've baked. I know Miss Myrtle down the street from me is going to miss my gifts of okra, tomatoes, and peppers now that the growing season is over. Oh, how her face lit up when I brought her those baskets of fresh-picked yummies! It doesn't take much. Let go of that excuse about time—there's just now. It's a relief that it is Now, it's freedom to be immersed in the moment, recognizing what is truly needed and not constrained by a schedule, real or imagined. Just stop and turn to someone right now—RIGHT NOW—and say "hi," smile with kindness, or get up and go outside and just do something, *anything*, to lift another person up. You will make their day and your own.

This Voice Sang Out

This entry from my journal written March 5, 2005, chronicles the first time I was asked to lead a chant. It was during my Integral Yoga Teacher Training when we had all gathered for a public *kirtan* and *satsang*.*

> "The room was full and I sat with eyes closed, taking in the sounds of the drums, rattles, guitar and voices chanting. I allowed the Witness to move in and push the ego gently aside. Then I heard my teacher, Nora *Vimala* Pozzi, whisper my name. I turned and looked at her, and she asked me to lead the closing chant. What an honor! I shifted gears and felt my heart race as this voice sang out of my mouth and the room full of people joined in. I was humbled and honored to have had that moment."

It really was that night and that song which gave me the voice to sing in public with confident grace. Indeed Japa Yoga, the Yoga of chanting as a tool for meditation, is one that has blessed me with profound moments of spiritual awakening, healing, connection with my guru, and has been instrumental in my work with teaching children's Yoga.

When we chant, we often sing songs in traditional Indian Sanskrit. This makes it easier, says master kirtanist Krishna Das, to not get attached to the meaning of the words, but rather to simply feel the overall vibration. After chanting you are filled with a sense of euphoria, peace, calm, and deep abiding in the Now. As a meditation, it is an effective tool for keeping the mind free from the myriad thoughts, so there is only the chant.

Early in my Teacher Training, when we were in Yogaville for a weekend intensive, I had come out of noon meditation and had my first heart-opening experience. As the sun broke out of the clouds, a chant filled my heart, *Om Namah Shivaya,* and transformed into a personal message. I still feel something in me shift when I sing this chant.

Breaking down chanting, we find that the simplest expression of the Cosmic Vibration is through the sound of OM. Sri Swami Satchidananda says:

> "OM is the sound of the Cosmic Vibration. The entire cosmos vibrates. Every cell vibrates. In fact, the whole universe is nothing but sound vibrations. The basic vibration is a hum, and the sum total of the universal vibration is also a hum. In between, there are fragments. All

the words, all the languages, all the various sounds that are created by the human beings or animals or even machines are smaller parts of this cosmic hum. Without that hum, there is nothing. To denote that cosmic hum, there should be a word. OM is the word that comes closest to representing that cosmic hum. The word OM itself is not the hum. It's the *name* of the hum."

During one of the darkest, most difficult challenges of my life, when I truly thought I could take no more, my car broke down on the highway late on a rainy, cold night. I arranged for a tow truck and waited for it to arrive. In that time I did not become agitated, stressed or angry. Yoga has taught me to adjust, adapt, and accommodate as best I can in every situation. So as I sat with gratitude that I had a Yoga blanket to cover my cold legs, a chant came to me like a dear friend and filled my head, my mind, my body, my heart, and I breathed deeply and let go.

Just like the horrible event that I had just come out of, and was still recovering from, what saved me through all of it was sound vibration through chanting. I sang to the chant and let myself sink into the darkness, and all I heard was *Om Sri Rama, Jaya Rama, Jaya Jaya Rama.* This mantra translates to in English: "Om and Victory to Rama (the Self within), Victory, Victory to Rama."

So, I then looked further and found that Rama was an Avatar who came here several thousand years ago. He came to show us how to live a Divine Life while in a human body. Gandhi recited this mantra for over 60 years! It is said this mantra will take you across the ocean of rebirth. It is recited to reduce negative karmic effects and is extremely healing. I find it fascinating that this was the mantra that came to me, and was such a dear friend through that most difficult time and taught me again how powerful sound vibration can be in shifting the mind to a place of peace from one of anguish.

Of all the six Branches in Yoga philosophy, Japa is the path of chanting or singing your prayers. And really, in order for any of the six Branches to truly be authentic, Bhakti Yoga is vital. Bhakti is the Yoga of Devotion. For when we open our hearts, when we allow ourselves to surrender to a higher power, then chanting takes on a whole new level of a deeply profound experience to realize the Self.

And what is Yoga if not that: to realize the true Self?

Kirtan is a gathering for Yogic chanting. *Satsang* is a gathering of a *sangha* (spiritual community) who have come together to hear a teaching relative to Yoga philosophy or living Yoga.

Devotion

LETTER TO MY GURU:

I thought I'd come visit you today
and feel your love run through me.
All around me I've heard the sound of water
running over rocks, leaves rattling in the trees,
and the sound of nature's silence.
I breathe in deeply and I hold your breath inside of me—
it fills me with life.
Before me the carpet is marked by my hands' path
as I prostrated to you, heart open.
My heart, my heart, sings with Bhakti Yoga—
It is your song.
As I close my eyes and sink into meditation,
I sit upon the cushion of your lap
and feel you holding me there.
We are one and now I know peace.
I thought I'd come home today, and sit with you,
and feel your love running through me.

I took a day to wander the hills of Satchidananda Ashram–Yogaville in Buckingham, Virginia, by myself. I stopped to listen, to breathe, and to connect to Source on an exquisite autumn day.

These are the gifts we can give ourselves.

What does it mean to experience Bhakti Yoga? What does it mean to open your heart to the Divine, to Source, to God? Outside of any mosque, temple, or church, open yourself to the Truth that we are all manifestations of Love, and there you will experience Bhakti Yoga. I explain to my Yoga kids that Bhakti Yoga is opening the heart to someone or something that inspires you to be greater than you already are.

Sri Swami Satchidananda is my guru. In his presence, which is everywhere, I am inspired to teach from my heart with total surrender to the Source of all that Yoga is. My classes are blissful and uplifting for anyone of any age, not because of me, but because of what I allow to move through me, and that is the Light of Love.

I took a day to wander by myself. I stopped to listen, to breathe, and to connect to Source on an exquisite autumn day.

These are the gifts we can give ourselves.

Reflections upon Pew Perching

As a child, growing up in the Brown Memorial Presbyterian Church in Baltimore City, it was certainly the reward of sugar cookies and Hawaiian Punch afterwards in the chapel hall that kept me patiently perched in my pew every Sunday morning. But in those years I somehow did hear the voice of God most dearly. It is now that I have come to believe, for myself, that God is neither man nor woman, but the Living Spirit within all of us. It is a treasured relationship I have found through living Yoga that continually guides and inspires me. It is in that that I found my calling to teach children and adults to connect with their own Inner Light. For children it is showing them how to be still and listen within, and to create that relationship with themselves. For adults it is a matter of being reminded to rediscover through surrendering anew to the Higher Self. Living Yoga, for me, is living in Spirit.

The voice of God is heard in each kind word, each offering of selfless service, each opportunity we have to show love to another. There are countless moments every day presented to us to offer a smile to a stranger, to gesture a touch of caring, to act for the benefit of another. Why else are we here? Why else are we here than to be the Living Spirit of Love? This is our greatest job in this life, my friends, to Love ourselves and all sentient beings unconditionally. If you surrender to anything, surrender to Love. Awaken your Living Spirit as you live through Yoga, and there you will abide in the Spirit of our united God.

Faith through Loss

It is the one thing we all know to be true, as true as the very breath we are now breathing, and that is that we all eventually die. No one wants to sit around thinking about it, planning for it, or giving it much thought until someone we know dies or becomes terminally ill. That's when life can seem to slow down, almost like a slo-mo moment in a movie, and in our heads we're thinking, "Is this really happening?" Sometimes the person who dies is no one we knew well, but we feel the pain for their loved ones, we empathize deeply with their suffering.

Death does not always make sense, especially when it's someone young, in the prime of their life. Death does not always come gently like a whisper in the night that takes away that last breath. Sometimes death is violent, sudden, and cuts through the core of you like a jolting shock. Sometimes death is a great relief when a loved one has suffered for a long time with disease and illness.

An old school friend of mine died after a years-long battle with breast cancer. I found myself thinking back on that time of high school and those people who were so much my reality back then. I thought about how I've grown as a person and wished I'd done some things differently. Her funeral was today, *this day* that I am writing this.

In Eastern Tibet an earthquake shook a small remote village, and I felt the anguish of His Holiness, the Dalai Lama, who so desperately wanted to visit and give blessings, but wasn't allowed access by the Chinese government. I have found my morning practice lately has been full of prayers for the dying, for all the sentient beings who are grief-stricken.

Death reminds us to Live.

Thus shall you see in all this fleeting world,
A star at dawn, a bubble in a stream,
A flash of lightening in a summer cloud,
A flickering lamp, a phantom, and a dream.

—THE BUDDHA
FROM THE DIAMOND SUTRA

Where Did My Practice Go?

In the classic Yoga teaching, *The Yoga Sutras of Patanjali*, it is written, "Practice becomes firmly grounded when well-attended for a long time, without break, and in all earnestness."

So the goal, then, is to have a daily meditation practice that is done in total devotion, with open-hearted reverence. It's not like you crawl onto the cushion as if it's something you *have to* do. It's not that you're sitting there thinking how great it is that you are sitting there. It is that you sit there, every day, feeling your mind empty and your heart open, free from the ego, free from the distractions of life.

But life happens, and we experience strings of crappy weather days, illness, schedule changes, and interruptions from our regularly-scheduled program impact the routine of practice. Without warning you wake up one day asking yourself, "Where did my practice go?" But, before that self-invoked wave of guilt washes over you, realize this as well—practice is made manifest through living it.

Even though the ultimate goal is to establish a solid practice of sitting meditation, the real test is to live your practice in your daily life. Living practice is living life as best you can with a gentle smile on your face to share with every person you see. Living practice is keeping your heart open to offer actions and words that reflect the depth of your faith born of your practice. Each morning as I meditate, I offer the vow of the Bodhisattva: "For as long as space endures, for as long as sentient beings exist, so shall I too remain to dispel the miseries of this world."

Once you start, hold fast to that commitment of daily practice, knowing that sacred time with yourself is a treasure so dear. Nurture it with all your radiant heart.

The Meaning of Thanksgiving

Holidays as a child were filled with traditions of family, of food, and music. The sound of my grandad playing old favorites on the piano, with everyone gathered in the living room, resonated joy throughout the house. The meal of fresh Eastern Shore oyster casserole, turkey, and all the rest of the feast live vividly in my mind, just as the river that ran by our home, carrying the seasons and memories of a time gone by.

As a vegetarian the last many years, the Thanksgiving holiday has shifted to one more about the blessing than the food. For in a nation resplendent with all manner of provisions to satisfy our tastes and tummy at any hour of the day, surely the truest meaning rooted in the Day of Thanks are the blessings of family, of community, of life itself.

All over the world cultures give thanks and bless the animal killed to feed their people—the Tibetans with the yak, the Native Americans with the buffalo, tribes in Africa with the game they hunt. And no part of that animal is wasted or taken for granted—the animal itself is a gift from the Earth. We have lost that connection.

This holiday is a time when you can stop and remind all who circle your table what a gift the animals are that lay before you, or how wondrous to savor the various bowls and platters of roots and fruits of the Earth. Do not gorge, but slow down to sincerely appreciate the offering of the food to share with your family.

As I grew up and moved away from home, family passed on, and their stories, music and laughter are still present at my small table on Thanksgiving. We fast on that day, filling our hours with prayer and quiet contemplation until dinner time when we break fast with a simple vegetarian meal. It is a tradition I hope my daughter will look back upon as I do, of childhood celebrations woven with the fabric of that time. Perhaps you may choose to skip the traditional turkey and find an alternative, or at the very least, opt for a free range turkey, sourced locally.

The holiday of Thanksgiving is based on faith, trust, and community with the native peoples of this land. The Native Americans have taught us through their way of life to step lightly on this Earth and to leave as small a footprint as we can in respect for all She provides. I bow in homage to the Native Americans, to the Europeans who bravely voyaged here, for the traditions woven through the holiday season that remind us to support our local community, to embrace our family unconditionally, and to be ever-grateful for all we are so blessed to have and to share.

The Gift of Nothing

In a world and in a time when we all have so much, I began to wonder if maybe, with all the things we do have, if something was missing. It is during the holiday season, when we begin making lists, that we are stumped by what to give all our loved ones, many of whom already have everything they need. Then a book inspired a thought: What if we gave each other the gift of nothing? For it is within the emptiness and simplicity of nothing that one can find everything.

And so, for you, I offer this box from which out of nothing I hope you will find everything you will ever need. This box holds the love of a friend, the peace of a snowy morning, the hope of sunshine after days of rain, a hand of support firm on your back, the embrace of understanding, a smile of joy, and all those very important things. May you trust that this box holds these with my blessing.

This thought came from the book, *The Gift of Nothing*, by Patrick McDonnell. I have read this book to my Yoga kids countless times. One year for Christmas I decided to buy lots of little boxes, and in each one I put a little note that said something like, "This box holds my love" or "This box is filled with healing." And I wrapped them in pretty paper and gave them to my family. It is a very powerful gift, to give a gift as big as your love, or friendship, or really anything that comes from your heart written on a note and placed inside an empty box.

If you were to give such a gift, what would your box hold?

Remind Me of What I Love

I read a missive from Carolyn Myss, medical intuitive and inspirational guru, with this title: *Remind Me of What I Love.* It struck me how often we do things, for the reason of "doing," but ultimately, are we doing what we love? Over time is it possible to become disengaged from what it is that we love? Even if our work is not our passion, we can create excitement in our lives for something that is. What is that one thing that, when you talk about it or think about it, makes you light up from head to toe? A deep inner joy for something? And yet, how easy it is to let that something slip away while focused on other "necessary" things. Some of us have yet to find their passion, some of us have forgotten what it is, and others live their passions daily.

That one thing that brings tears to my eyes and fully opens my heart in the most joy-filled way is teaching children Yoga. I can't think of anything else I do that makes me happier and more complete as a person. As I look for teaching gigs, I sometimes ponder if I should be doing something different. And then I am reminded of what I love—my joy of teaching Yoga to children, especially during the weeks of Yoga camp. It is something I am not ready to let go of any time soon.

We all have choices to make, sacrifices to make, a livelihood to maintain. At the end of the day we can still ask ourselves "What is it I most love?" See where that question takes you—meditate on the answers as they come up, then create ways to bring that into your life in whatever way you can. To live a life doing *what you most love to do* is to live a life fulfilled. Perhaps that is the greatest reward at the end of the day. The paycheck is secondary.

Teacher–Student

Even what appears to be ordinary can have extraordinary effects that are far-reaching, beyond anything you could have imagined.

Many years ago I taught a mid-day class on Thursdays. It was a class that I had carried from my own studio to another studio. It was a class mostly attended by people who were retired or worked from home. But one day a beautiful young woman came to class, and did so for quite a while. I marveled at her fluid movement in and out of *asanas* (poses), and her bright, youthful energy. Then she moved to Washington, DC, and I didn't see her for a long time.

Little did I know that that noon Hatha class had a profound impact on her. In fact, she went on to become an Integral Yoga teacher, studying in Yogaville, where she now works. I now have the great delight of coordinating with her when I plan events there, like retreats and Yoga camp stays. So, it was a true gift when I was in Yogaville with the Richmond Integral Yoga Teacher Trainees in our morning Hatha class, that who should be our teacher but my former student! She led an exquisite class and she mentioned me as her "stepping stone" that launched her into this new life of teaching and living Yoga! It was such a profound moment, a moment of witnessing the effects that my own teaching had had on one student.

This was not the first time I have seen my work have a positive influence on a student or a student's family, but this was the first time I had a student become a teacher who could then *teach me*. In the ocean of life, we are all pebbles with the potential to throw ourselves into any number of situations and relationships which create a ripple effect. Whether positive or negative, the outcome is up to both you and the recipient of your actions and words. Never doubt that we are all connected, and we all have the power to change one another in infinite ways.

It was a deeply humbling moment to have taken this Hatha class with my student. I saw the ripple I caused in her life come back and touch me, bringing tears to my eyes, opening my heart wide, and resonating the vibration of Yoga throughout both our lives.

IN DEEP REVERENCE TO MY BELOVED STUDENT, SHANKARI.

Planting the Seeds of Meditation

The image is this: A farmer, anxious for his crops to grow, went out in the field to tug on the new sprouts. This is obviously not the way to get what he wanted any faster—in fact he would harm the progress already made.

A student once asked me how to approach meditation when her mind is constantly racing from one thought to the next. If you want to manifest something, you have to be a mindful farmer.

The mind is like a fertile field. The intention of meditation, and the creating of the space in which to do so, is like clearing the field. First, the weeds of distraction are pulled up—this may be actually clearing out a room to create a meditation space, even if just a corner. This may also apply to your physical body. Clearing the physical body to allow for focus and stillness requires a *sattvic* diet—pure foods that are harvested from the Earth—organic, fresh fruits and vegetables, whole grains, seeds, nuts, beans, and legumes. Removing the heavy meats, processed foods, alcohol, and sugar is a major step towards clarity of mind. So now, imagine your field is cleared—you have created the space for meditation, and you've modified your diet to a healthier one.

The next step, then, is to plant the seeds of meditation with a daily intention of spending a specific amount of time sitting. The seeds are really your intention. You water this intention with actual practice, and you offer the warmth of the sun by embracing your meditation with an open heart. Germination happens here, but you've only just sprouted.

The last piece to truly make your practice grow and thrive is *dharma*—reading the teachings of your guru, from whatever faith or philosophy inspires you. But you cannot sit like an advertisement in lotus posture, with hands on knees in a *mudra*, and expect to tug on the sprouts to make your practice suddenly manifest. Sprouts are merely what's visible. A vital plant needs roots that go deep. It takes time, it takes devoted effort, it takes discipline, and patience. Once you start practicing daily meditation, slowly the first sprouts of stillness arise. Over time your practice becomes part of who you are—you literally live your faith, your meditation, your practice in your life, and it integrates into your very essence of being.

At some point the altar of sacred images, incense, and candles is carried within your heart. You may not become a Buddha or reach enlightenment in this lifetime, but the closest thing to that is to carry the altar, carry the *dharma*, carry the practice within your heart and live it out loud to the best of your ability for the benefit of all sentient beings. That is when you're able to look back on your field and realize it has yielded a most abundant crop.

It starts with you allowing stillness and silence to enter your life. From there your practice will grow. Remember, we all hold the seeds, you just need to plant them.

Three Little Things
That Make a Big Difference

How can finding peace within your Self seem so complicated? Why do we push ourselves all day, day after day, until we are sick or so disconnected that we don't recognize ourselves? Life is simple. *We* complicate it. Connecting to peace within ourselves is also really simple—we just have to train ourselves to stop.

Really?

Yes. *Just Stop!* Like that red light up ahead: start braking now before you have to slam on the brakes. Those breaks are saving you from speeding ahead, running on and on and on until you run out of gas or crash.

Gracious, this sounds so serious!

Um . . . It is.

Connecting to your Self everyday should be like religion, or brushing your teeth, or drinking water. This one-on-one time—you with your Self—is paramount to your well-being. It is so simple. It just takes doing three things:

1) **Get Still**, which means sit down and don't move. Pick a happy place in your home or outside where you won't be disturbed.

2) **Get Quiet**. Shhhh! No talking, unless you feel the need to talk out loud to yourself. That's perfectly fine at first, but then let silence wash over you.

3) **Breathe**. Yes, I know you were already breathing, but now you are breathing mindfully, which means you are aware of your breath. Just breathe. Focus all your attention on the in-breath and the out-breath, until you find a rhythm.

How long do you have to sit there? Start with a minimum of three to five minutes (about 60 slow, mindful breaths). In an entire day the average person takes 23,040 breaths. If you think counting 60 breaths is tedious, be glad you weren't the person who counted their breaths for an entire day so the rest of us could know that fascinating fact.

Now, as you get into a habit of sitting every day, you can take this deeper with self-inquiry by adding a journal. Take time to write down your thoughts and feelings. The more you connect with your Self, the stronger a relationship you forge. You will begin to seek out this time, recognizing the benefits of self-inquiry, introspection, of stopping and being still. You will crave this time alone with your Self, because it will awaken in you something you have longed for—*peace.*

Peace is a seed within us all, but it requires that stillness and silence to really grow. And who knows what the flower of peace looks like within you? Only you can discover that. That's part of the magic of meditation—it is your experience and yours alone. Nurture it, give it attention, and watch how it opens up a sweet silence within your spirit.

Catching Yourself

It was during a class soon after the earthquake of 2010 that I began to notice the intensified anxiety around me. This only worsened the following year after the wrath of hurricane Irene, which left millions of people without power for over a week. It is times like those, when events happen outside of our control, that we fear helplessness, reacting with anxiety and stress. In fact, if you look carefully, there has been an increase in natural disasters and tragedies of various proportions all over the planet. Mother Earth is changing, her vibration is rising, and much is being affected as a result. Our unrelenting hand in exhausting her resources, drilling and polluting, only exacerbates what is happening.

As passengers on this amazing planet, we are collectively sharing in and witnessing a time of great change. Polarities are widening, as we have seen in world politics and cultural divisions. A sense of frantic seems to consume our society in which we already felt such a sense of hurriedness. There is so much to do in so little time, and yet we keep scheduling more to do.

In a preschool Yoga class, with about 20 three-years-olds, I begin each class taking big breaths, sweeping our arms up over our heads in a big circle. I have taught them that "Your breath is your friend. When lightning crashes or grown-ups are fighting, and you are feeling scared—take a deep breath and know that everything is okay. When mom or dad drop you off at daycare and you're feeling sad inside—take a deep breath and know they love you very much. When you are angry and feel like you could throw something, or hurt somebody, or say something really mean—take a deep breath and let your anger go. Your breath is your friend."

So this particular day, I took this teaching to another level. Sometimes, you have to catch yourself. So I asked them to clap their hands together. I said, "Now you've caught yourself! Look inside your clasped hands, do you see yourself? Oh, my, that is one angry person, terribly angry. What should we do? Take some deep breaths! Peek inside and let's see . . . Are we doing better? Yes!" Sometimes, friends, we must *all* learn to catch ourselves and take a peek inside.

As the vibration of our planet rises and we continue to lead very full lives, it is essential that we learn to catch ourselves. You have a choice—you can choose to continue to feel the anxiety and stress of this vibration or you can learn to tune into it and rise up to meet it. The first step is to open your self up to Spirit and release so much of the over-doing, over-scheduled living.

Much of this is about balance in our lives, but even more importantly, it is about waking up to what is really happening here—to why we are really here.

Hatha Yoga offers you the opportunity to be present on your mat, stretching your body to motivate the movement of *chi* or *prana* or life force. *Yoga nidra* (deep relaxation) then allows time for you to go deeper and motivate the subtle, pervasive, essential *prana* of breath through tensing and releasing, then surrendering to a time of just being. I know that a lot of the Hatha that people gravitate towards is more active and power-driven, but I urge you to also discover the slower, more easeful styles of Hatha, such as Restorative, Gentle, Integral, or Yin classes, especially those that include meditation.

The two most important, root practices of Hatha Yoga are *pranayama* (breathing exercises) and meditation. Here you can sit in stillness and silence, following the breath, and catching yourself. It might surprise you that despite all that your life is, your True Self is essentially very peaceful, very calm, very joyful, very loving, very grateful, and very compassionate.

To truly tune yourself to Mother Earth's rising vibration, try meditating outdoors—sky gaze, bird watch, hike, breathe with the trees, root yourself into the Earth, and feel her vibration with bare feet against the ground. She is asking us to surrender to Love, the greatest vibration of all. This is our work, and it requires that we catch our Self, calm down, sit, and breathe.

Stop! Breathe!

Here are lessons worth sharing from two children I taught privately.

The first student was a young boy with anger management issues. We will call him Z. I was teaching him to breathe as a tool to feel in control when the world around him felt out of control. Each Yoga pose we held for a count of ten slow breaths. This helped him to be in his body—present and calm. We talked about his anger, and I told him that he is not an angry person. Rather, the anger is like a monster inside of him, making him lose control, but Z is the superhero who can slay the monster with his breath.

After several private lessons, the breathing wasn't helping when he was in a full-blown tantrum. I asked Z to draw me a picture of his monster. What he showed me were three distinct drawings on a single page, each one was a different shape—a triangle, a square and a circle. They each had a made-up name associated with them, and a color too—yellow, orange, and red (I found it fascinating that he recognized the stages of his own anger as it grew and overpowered him).

So I asked him, "With which monster is your breathing *not* going to help?"

He said "The red one."

"That is right, because by the time you are *that* mad, you have lost the game and the monster wins. Where could your breath really help?"

He pointed to the Yellow shape.

"Yes, at the moment you start to feel overwhelmed, that things aren't going your way, start to breathe. As you breathe in, squeeze your hands shut. And when you breathe out, open your hands, letting those feelings go. Keep breathing in and out with your hands until you, the superhero Z, can slay the yellow monster and win the game." I told him that when he gets red monster angry he never gets what he wants, but if he can overcome his anger, he just might. But even if he doesn't, he still won the battle with the angry monster and he can feel like the *super*-superhero that I know he can be.

The second student was a little girl, just five years old, who we will call C. She had anxiety (which I determined from my own experience with a daughter with Asperger's that she had early signs of Sensory Integration Disorder). Certain clothing felt funny, she has a tendency towards perfectionism, and she was easily overwhelmed. So, again, we began classes where each pose was held for 10 slow breaths. For an active little girl, I was pleased to see her so calm on the mat, breathing her breaths, her eyes closed while in each Yoga pose. I also used the mantra that her breathing was a tool to help her feel in control when the world around her felt out of control. In some ways having that one-on-one, concentrated focus on one activity seemed to be a relief to her. She really enjoyed the tensing and releasing at the end as we went into *Yoga nidra* (deep relaxation).

For C, I asked her to use a "stop sign" as her tool for anxiety. When she begins to feel overwhelmed, she can put up a hand and verbalize that she needs a moment. This lets her caretakers know what is happening inside of her, that she feels afraid that she can't keep up, or that the situation is overwhelming, and she is asking for help. I asked her parents to also use the "stop sign" as a tool for the whole family to slow down and take a calmer pace, especially during more stressful times of the day, like getting ready for school. Also, for C, this was a way for her take control of the situation and honor her own needs. Breathing to calm down and reconnect to her body, while having the adults in her life know what she needs, gives her a tool for self-management.

I share these two client stories with you because we can learn from them how to better be in this world. A slower pace, a calmer approach, releasing the urge to push and rush. And, if we have children, to recognize the influence our behavior has on their well-being. Take time in your day for everyone to relax and hang out with no organized activities, just chilling out. But, when life is happening and a lot is going on, don't forget the "stop sign."

Breathe. Breathe. Breathe. Slow down and give yourself or your kids a hug and show them—remind yourself—how to be more present.

The Golden Moment

We stand up from our cushions, our altars, our places of peace, and the security of home. We walk out into the day of traffic, meetings, shopping, driving, and seemingly endless doing. How do we maintain that center of peace we evoke in our practice with this barrage of sound, motion, emotion, and activity?

I was driving home, feeling a mother's exhilarated anticipation of freedom of a few hours *alone*. I was listening to a mix-tape of old songs and found my mind had wandered off into the "what's next, who to call, where do I need to go, and when" runaway mind-train. I got off the exit and sat at the traffic light. The red light brought me to a "STOP." I took this as a sign, literally and metaphorically.

I noticed again the music that had been lost in the background, Simon & Garfunkel singing, "I've got nothing to do today but smile." And I smiled. I looked at the car in front of me. The license plate read: BEHAPPY. As the smile tickled my face, those words sunk in, and a clarity rose like a new-day sun deep within the center of my being. I felt HAPPY, and I drove back home with this very PRESENT GOLDEN MOMENT feeling inside. All the crap, all the clutter in my mind, was cleansed by the simple acts of smiling and being very much *in the Now*.

This Golden Glow of Glory—LIFE—is NOW. And NOW is exactly where we are meant to be. Quoted from *The Golden Present: Daily Inspirational Readings* by Sri Swami Satchidananda:

> "Always remember the golden present. Never miss it. A happier life is not given to you by someone else. Not even God can give you a happier life. Remember that. Happiness is in you. If you take care not to lose it, it is always there."

Throughout our days there are these SIGNS that make us STOP, that bring us back to the GOLDEN PRESENT—license plates, some bit of an overheard conversation, a book title, a great blue heron streaking across the sky, a paw print in a dried mud puddle.

Yesterday morning I opened the front door to feel the weather of the day. I took a deep breath and scanned the yard as if to verify all was as I left it. A neighbor's garden hose caught my eye, and then a flicker of green at his flowering bushes. What was that? Being more awake and very PRESENT MO-

MENT, I realized it was a hummingbird. It flew a straight line across the yard to the snapdragons blooming in pots on either side of my steps. I stood with the door open, silently witnessing this hummingbird's morning drink.

These are the SIGNS. These are our reminders to STOP. Look around at the details of this magnificent world around us.

BE HERE NOW—the MOMENT is GOLDEN.
SMILE, friend. We are BREATHING LIFE.

Mind-Full-Ness

Being present in the space of each perfect moment of life is to walk the path of Buddhas, Bodhisattvas, Gurus, and Yogis throughout the course of time. It is not difficult to begin the journey. It is not difficult to tune in and notice that, as you are walking, you feel the Earth beneath your feet, sensing the ground as grass, gravel, or sand. Allow the presence of yourself in each moment, in which you have the opportunity to say to yourself, "I am washing my hands" or "I am sipping my tea" or "I am walking the dog." When you are working, your mind is focused on the task at hand. When you are driving, you are aware of the road and the cars. How can you be present if you are driving and talking on the phone?

There is so much to distract you and so much to tempt you from being mindful and present. To truly embrace life we must train ourselves anew to turn away from these distractions. Try not to answer the phone when you are driving, or reading to your child, or talking to a friend who is visiting you. Turn off the television and walk away from the computer and truly *be home* so you can be present and available to your loved ones (including yourself).

Stop *now* and take a deep breath. Be consciously aware of the expansion of breath filling your lungs and your body. Now exhale—*aaahhhh!* Perfect moment. Present moment. You are alive.

When you eat, try eating in silence. Allow yourself to be present with your food. The events of your day do not sit down with you at the table—just you and your plate of food. You do not want to put into your mouth forkfuls of despair, worry, or stress. You simply want to eat your food. When you put a forkful of salad in your mouth, really experience all the textures and tastes, knowing that it was the sun, rain, and Earth that grew those vegetables, and they become part of you as you swallow. Imagine all of Nature is on your plate as you eat and nourish your body. Choosing foods that are *sattvic*, pure and close to the Earth, is not only healthy for you, but essential to a mind that can stay clear and present.

Imagine how your life can be transformed just by making a few, subtle, conscious changes, like driving mindfully, being home and present, or eating with purposeful awareness. Just to start there is to begin to live Yoga. It is to take the mat with you through your daily life. This is your journey. We all share the road in our own way, but ultimately we are all moving in the same direction.

The question remains, are your eyes open? Are you here? Are you present in this *now* moment?

Take a deep breath. Exhale. *Ahhhh!*

Visualize the space of your heart. Close your eyes. Take another deep breath and exhale from your heart. Awaken! This is *Now*, and it is the perfect moment to embrace in *Namaste*.

Listening Walk

No talking.
Walk slowly and mindfully.
Have no expectations.
Leave your phone at home.

When you go on a Listening Walk you can be anywhere—a neighborhood, a park, or woods. The key is to be a witness to all of life around you, soaking in the senses of what you see, smell, and hear. As the weather warms with the coming spring, you may notice the sun feels warmer on your skin, the breeze is gustier, and the natural world is more alive. It can be fun to take your Listening Walk with a friend, and together gather as many threads from your mindful journey, then afterward discuss—weaving a tapestry of the experience.

A Listening Walk is very much a kind of meditation, because your focus is clear, and you are so mindfully present. As you begin, pay attention first to your breath and your steps. Breathe in and take one step, breathe out and take another step. This slows your pace as you begin to let go and become two big ears.

Listen to the layers of sound—a car tire hitting a pot hole, a jogger breathlessly running by, a woodpecker rapping on a dead branch of a tree, the wind snapping a flag, a dog barking in a distant yard, or the soulful howl of a train whistle. All the while you are walking—breathing in, taking a step, breathing out, taking a step, with full awareness expanding to take in the world around you.

Connecting to Nature

When was the last time you went for a walk? How about a walk in the woods? How about a walk with a child in the woods?

Many of us recall our childhood days of playing in our neighborhoods for hours on end—climbing trees, collecting feathers, riding bikes, building forts, and letting our imaginations immerse us in the fantastical world of childhood. Increasingly, studies and books, like *Last Child in the Woods* by Richard Louv, educators, and parents are documenting and commenting on the growing crisis of new generations of children that have lost touch with the natural world in a very technology-focused culture. Yet, we know that after a few hours or a day spent outside, we are healthier, happier, and less stressed. Nature feeds our souls.

Some of my daughter's first toys were pine cones, feathers, and rocks. She and I are adventurers. I raised her to see the world as a wild place to explore. With camera, magnifying glass, binoculars, and pockets to fill, she and I spent countless hours outdoors on great expeditions.

Get motivated to climb a tree, go for a hike, put your hands in the dirt and plant something. Practice Hatha Yoga in a park, hug trees, and feel Nature's air conditioning of a cool breeze in the shade on a hot day.

Open your windows, walk away from all the electronics, drive with the windows down, look up and maybe you'll see a red tail hawk circling the sky, or look down and see what little insects are making their way through the lawn. Look how the light breaks through the clouds or illuminates the leaves in the trees. Take your shoes off and jump into a mud puddle, or walk barefoot on the Earth—feel that grounding, nourishing energy healing your body. Take deep breaths, face to the sky, arms outstretched, and smile.

Connecting to Our Mother

I went outside this morning to connect to Mother Earth and Father Sky. I laid down a quilt and I laid down my body. I aligned my cells with Mother Earth, I connected my spirit to Father Sky. I watched the clouds, I watched and heard the birds.

I've been holding on to a deep, inner quiet. There's a calm in our world if you stop to feel it. Nature shows it so clearly.

Its winter, time to slow down, to be still, to be quiet, and to reflect.

We have gotten too busy, too lost in screens and electronics, too controlled by schedules, hyper-doing, hyper-thinking, and we have forgotten to live. We have forgotten to touch that still point within and to breathe with awareness.

Lie down on the Earth, sit by a river, climb a mountain, gaze at the stars, cloud watch. Close your eyes and feel the sun on your face, watch the squirrels play and the leaves dance. Connect to nature and recognize your Self as one with it. Breathe, experience, be aware, and know that you are nothing without it—without Nature.

We are all connected: human, animal, plant, river, rock, earth. We all breathe, we all love, and we are all alive in this *now*, perfect moment.

Nature is Medicine

Summertime is such an incredible invitation to get outside and play—hiking, biking, walking, canoeing, swimming, meditating, reading, painting, hugging trees. There is *so* much to do, and you don't have to be active, you can just sit with it. Have you ever hugged a tree? Have you ever sat and *listened* to a tree? One of the most primal acts is to communicate with our natural world, for it has so much to tell us.

One summer I had been suffering with anemia, and despite my weakness, I went to Yogaville to lead my annual women's retreat. I knew this would be a time to embrace quiet, calm, and a more easeful pace, which was just what I needed. The day for our slow float in inner tubes down the James River arrived, and I was very hesitant about going. I kept worrying about my safety, and if I could manage such an activity. When I told the women in our group that I was considering staying behind, their responses were filled with disappointment. They wanted to share this experience with me. So with their support and our collective enthusiasm, I decided to join them. We headed off to the river on a beautiful summer day.

As soon as I plopped myself onto that inner tube and felt the cool water, the warm breeze, the community of women all peaceing out and blissful, I knew I had made the best decision. In fact, by the time our two-hour float was over, I felt rejuvenated and refreshed. My take-away from the entire retreat experience was that Nature is Medicine. As that summer continued, I hiked, swam, and experienced the outdoors in so many ways with my Yoga camp kids, on my own camping trips, and even on daily dog walks.

No matter where you find it, Nature is there for you to feel connected, nurtured, and healed.

Openness Beyond Attachment

Look at your house. What do you see? Do you start a mental list of all the things wrong, that need to be fixed or replaced, or do you see a place where you safely, comfortably, gratefully abide? Just as in relationships, when asked how you are getting along, do you answer with all that isn't working, or do you find some positive things to share? The more you look, the more you will see the positive or negative in your mind.

The negative comes from the mind that judges, fixates and labels. The practice of meditation is there for you to rise above this monkey mind. You can use the power of breath, silence, and stillness to open yourself beyond the mind, beyond the pain body, beyond whatever situation or person is affecting you.

If you aren't happy with your house, you might chronically say to yourself, "Oh, this house needs this and that done!"

Sit down in your house. Find a favorite cozy spot. Close your eyes, and breathe deeply. Allow your breath to expand space within you. Know that it is only the labels, attachments, and judgments you are putting out there that make this home such a problem. Your house is fine, just as it is. Release, and feel this deeply. Of course, the *Feng Shui* guru in me has a caveat, to say here that if your home is toxic to your well-being, then you should make modifications to improve the situation. Always give yourself permission to remedy a toxic situation that is causing you undue suffering in any realm of your life.

Much like in a relationship, if you are struggling, and your partner is fixated on what's wrong with you, and you are fixated on what is wrong with them, surely no good will come of that. The truth is you are both deserving of love and respect. Sit down together, holding hands, without words. Close your eyes. Breathe deeply together and feel the space grow within you to allow the qualities of perfection to arise to truthfully see each other, and release all the rest. Sometimes though, the truth reveals that it is healthier to move on. Honor yourself above all else.

But practice is a discipline requiring a commitment to apply yourself with total presence, allowing space to arise, to bloom, to expand within. The practice of silent, still meditation will let you release the pain body, release whatever it is you thought was wrong. In reality all is as it should be and all is well . . . mostly.

Attachment

In the *Yoga Sutras of Patanjali* translation and commentary by Sri Swami Satchidananda, Book 2 section 3 says, "Ignorance, egoism, attachment, hatred, and clinging to bodily life are the five obstacles." Each of these five are given in order as they occur. It continues, "[With] ignorance of self, egoism comes. Because of egoism there is attachment to things for the ego's selfish pleasure. Because sometimes the things we are attached to do not come or are taken away, hatred for those who got in our way comes in. And finally because we are attached to things and are afraid of death, there is clinging to life in the body."

Attachment begins early in life and is the cause of so much suffering. In relationships we are emotionally attached to our friends and loved ones, even pets. My little cockatiel, Tony, gave very little to me, but I loved him, cared for him, and in the end when he died I buried him in the yard with loving-kindness. He never asked anything of me—I just loved and gave of my time to ensure his well-being. We do this for many of our friends and pets too—care for them, love them, and look for very little in return. The fact that someone considers you a friend seems enough. They are kind to you, considerate and perhaps offer you something that makes you feel you understand yourself better or more deeply being with them. Yet, there is attachment here and you know it exists when that friend or loved one is suddenly gone. Maybe you become resentful of their leaving, angry that they have chosen to move away, go back to school, or perhaps they are terminally ill. It may not be as extreme as hatred, but you may find you start distancing yourself from them as the time of their departure approaches.

Yoga teaches us to be in the moment and live in the now without looking back or looking forward. As I tell the kids in Yoga camp, "What happened before is a memory, what comes next is a dream, all we have is now so we might as well enjoy it!" Indeed, it is a tough lesson to learn, non-attachment. It means accepting the relationships in our lives for just what they are right now. When someone is leaving, for whatever reason, we continue to offer ourselves with loving-kindness to help or be there in whatever way they might need. Trust that the connection you have will surpass time, distance, even this lifetime.

Non-attachment eases the negative influences of the ego to allow resentment, anger, despair to diminish so that your True Self can shine through.

Your True Self transcends the ego and embraces all your relationships with an openness, freedom, love, and trust that abides in the moments that you share together. When you are apart there is no sense of clinging to some future outcome. Like a morning glory at dawn that blooms fully, open to the receptive moment of life, and then as the energy fades, it closes in. The morning glory is not attached to the sun rising every morning, but when it does it responds. Nor is the flower attached to the sun's duration or the inevitable rise of the moon when the flower folds its petals. The flower simply responds, present and receptive. As humans we can relate to the flower by being responsive, aware, accepting, and present. We find moments when, beyond ego and all its attachments, we can abide in our True Self and just be.

La Pura Vida

I went on vacation to Puntarenas, Costa Rica, with my family. Let me put this into perspective—that in all my adult life I have not once gone off on a family vacation of just *my* household. Previously I vacationed with my parents and siblings, often with my daughter and partner. Add to that, this was the first time in nearly twenty years of being a business owner that I took more than a week off without doing *any* work, including checking e-mail, the news, or social media. And it was liberating!

In Costa Rica we never heard anyone yelling or acting irritated or being aggressive. Oh, except one lady yelling at a white face monkey for stealing her strawberries at the beach in Manuel Antonio National Park, and that was pretty funny. This is a country with no military and hardly any police presence. This is a nation without guns. If a line was long, everyone just waited patiently. After all, what's the rush? *Pura Vida!*

As we traveled through little towns and along highways that were never more than two lanes, the drivers used short beeps of the horn to communicate cooperatively, maneuvering in a most amazing maze of navigation through some very tight spots. In restaurants ordering food, it could take up to an hour to be served, but it was always *muy delicioso* and served with so much simple joy. These are a humble people, embracing their motto: *la Pura Vida*—the pure life.

Pastel-painted concrete houses with tin roofs were the most common abode, and these couldn't have been more than 3–4 room houses with covered porches that served as their family room. The weather there is nearly always in the 80's during the day, so their lifestyle doesn't change much from month to month. But due largely to their simple living, contented mind-set, and the near absence of institutionalized violence, HappyLivingIndex.org ranked Costa Rica #1 as the happiest nation on earth.

What is impeding our ability to do that in our own lives? What if we tried to slow life down to live the Pure Life, *la Pura Vida*? Here in America we drive fast, eat and cook fast, do fast Yoga, and even can't wait for a natural birth and opt for C-sections to fit in with busy work schedules, and then we have a fast maternity leave. Think of all the things you have sped up in your own life. Americans are on hyper speed. Let's you and I change that!

Our lifestyle is driving us to be mentally and physically sick. We are stressed out and filled with anxiety because of the pace at which we try to live our lives, and it simply is not sustainable, nor is it as enjoyable as it could be.

From the moment you wake up, move slower and more mindfully. Sit an extra five minutes in your morning meditation. Sip your coffee or tea while enjoying the view from your window. Eat without a phone or television, or even a conversation, and truly enjoy your meal. Slow down your work day to really appreciate what it is you are doing with greater awareness and presence. Put your phone down and put it on airplane mode for a few hours. Drive patiently and courteously. Read a book! Pick up the phone and call friends instead of hiding behind text and e-mail. What else would change for you personally if you slowed down and tried a little more *Pura Vida?*

New Perspectives

Mary Oliver writes in her book of essays, *Upstream*, "When I was a child, living in a small town surrounded by woods and a winding creek—woods more pastoral than truly wild—my great pleasure, and my secret, was to fashion for myself a number of little houses. They were huts really, made of sticks and grass, maybe a small heap of fresh leaves inside. There was never a closure but always an open doorway, and I would sit just inside, looking out into the world."

This passage struck me for two reasons. One—I was such a child, building nature architectures and hiding from the world in order to gain a silent, uninterrupted perspective from wherever I was perched. Two—it is at this time of the year (summer) when my internal perspective shifts forward into the year ahead. Leaping like a frog, my mind hops between the many events already planned, mostly work-related, that I am looking forward to—retreats, teacher trainings, summer camp, and family occasions.

Generally, I try to stay in the present moment, focused and mindful, but lately I find myself more scattered, like the last of the leaves trying to find a place to land. There seems to be so much uncertainty, so much despair and deep concern about our collective future. How do we respond?

Make a habitat of peace, of light, of joy, of love in your own life. Strengthen it with resolve and conviction so that the foundation is sturdy. Keep the doors to your heart and mind open to whatever comes, fair weather or foul. Perch yourself so you are ready to help, to guide, to inspire those around you. Throw open the window to your inner Light to illuminate the world anew. For even the smallest of lights from the tiniest of openings can guide the lost from the darkest woods of their own souls.

Learning to Just Be

August is a funny month. It's when Yoga camp is finished and I'm gearing up for the next school year of classes. The first week, I was overwhelmed with a fatigue that knocked me down—in bed for days, unable to really do much of anything but sleep, read, and meditate. And that was it. Letting go of doing was harder than anything else I did leading up to this slower and quieter time of my year.

By the second week of August, I let go and found myself floating, with doing and not doing, but not really worrying about being so damned productive every day. My accomplishments included picking okra out of the garden, driving the kids to the movies, journaling for hours, cooking a ridiculous amount of food to put up for winter, and taking the dogs for meandering walks. But those were meaningful and worthwhile moments for sure, though they certainly weren't my usual work-saturated days.

When my daughter's school year resumed, I would drop her off and return home to face an empty house. I spent hours on the back porch with my thoughts and my journal and no agenda, other than to be present. September tends to be a slow transition into the fall teaching schedule for my business and I am grateful for that easeful time, content with my days and at peace with my Self, doing and not doing, being mindfully aware that whatever I choose to do or not is okay and is enough.

Deprogramming myself from this culture of push-do-go-run-sweat and drop-exhausted-at-the-end is crazy to let go of, as much as it is crazy to live. I was finally able to just be content, being okay with what is in any given moment, though just for a couple of weeks. And why do we need an excuse, like summer, to take a break? Let's find those pockets in our everyday lives to sit, to be still, to get quiet inside, and breathe deeply into the *just-being* of life.

My Autism Family

As my teenage daughter paraded around the living room, wearing a plastic Viking helmet and donning red, round hippy sunglasses while dancing to music, I looked to see my boyfriend's son laughing hysterically at nonsensical YouTube videos, and I thought, "This is perfect."

I had no need to correct anyone for odd behavior, for not acting their age, and I had no need to judge these unique kids at all. Here, in my family, I can relax and let each of our children just be his or her quirky, autistic self.

With a terrific sense of humor, with a view of the world more sensitive than most, the earth is populated with these magical, amazing beings who feel more, see more, hear more, taste more, and generally experience life more intensely.

It is a joy to find places where you can just be yourself and not feel criticized or measured by some inane societal standard. It is a relief to find someone who also has an autistic child, who relates to the level of patience, compassion, and love required to raise a special-needs person. In a society that pushes for you to be cool, popular, performing at peak level, excessively successful, and socially in the "in" crowd, families with special needs kids have to navigate around all of that and redefine success, relationships, and performance on a daily basis.

Why does it take labeling someone with a condition like autism for us to learn to accept differences, when really, if we are honest, we all are a little different. And in a world where people thrive on climbing to the top, being the most socially accepted, and being a part of a herd, I'd choose to walk to the beat of my own drum and let my freak flag fly happily. My daughter has taught me how beautiful the view is if you shift your perspective to see the world through the lens of her red, round hippy glasses.

Childhood Lost

And Deering's Woods are fresh and fair,
  And with joy that is almost pain
My heart goes back to wander there,
  And among the dreams of the days that were,
    I find my lost youth again.
And the strange and beautiful song,
  The groves are repeating it still:
"A boy's will is the wind's will,
  And the thoughts of youth are long,
    long thoughts."

—Henry Wadsworth Longfellow

For many of us, childhood was a long and resplendent journey filled with make-believe, cardboard box houses, fairy tales, playing with the kids in the neighborhood until the evening street lights came on, skinned knees, riding bikes without helmets, and roller skating without knee and elbow pads. Childhood was an adventure that allowed for outdoor exploration, figuring out how to interact with other kids without parental intervention, falling down without an immediate Band-Aid, independent play that lasted for hours with incredibly innovative, made-up games with other kids—or alone.

When any of us return to our hometowns, to that street where we recall those early, formative years, spilling out like pennies from our pockets for candy at the corner store, we are awash in the sentiment of a time immersed in a seemingly endless innocence. Childhoods now don't seem like childhoods then. Where has that gone? When did childhood become so abbreviated?

I have noticed the increasing number of kids in the 3rd and 4th grades who seem jaded and almost annoyed with the idea of being taken on an imaginary adventure with silly animals and fun songs. I don't remember this when I started teaching kids Yoga back in the early 2000's, but I really notice it now. It saddens me that make-believe and childhood innocence could be finished at the age of eight or nine. In these years I have been teaching, many of my students started with me when they were five years old, even as young as two. Some grew up with me and became camp counselors, even lead teachers. I feel like I am their Yoga Mamma, and I have seen them develop and grow up learning to live Yoga.

I'd like to think that my classes reinforced their childhood wonder of imaginary places by being told stories about Farmer Brown and Mrs. Brown, Slinky the Fox, Old Brown Cow, the frogs down at the Swampy Swamp. My approach to teaching is not just to have the kids learn to connect body and breath in poses, how to breathe deeply and mindfully, how to relax and find peace in meditation, but to also excite their imaginations and share that experience with them. *To play.* I have no issue with pretending to be six years old again, to get down low and see the world through their eyes. Indeed, there are adults that never entirely left that innocence of childhood behind and can easily slip into imaginative play.

Do we point fingers and place blame? What would that prove or explain? Is part of it that we parents need our kids to grow up faster? I see some kids who are lucky to attend certain schools that foster a more wonder-filled, play-centered learning environment that nurtures the child. I also see parents who encourage the extension of childhood with how they interact with their children, but there are others who push hard and expect a lot and overschedule activities until the child has no time left for independent play. My daughter, born in 1998, grew up gravitating towards books and Nature, whereas kids now are handed i-Pads and electronic devices to entertain them.

It's a different time, a new world, and childhood seems to have suddenly transformed. I am not writing this from a place of judgment, but more of conjecture. Ultimately, it comes down to us, the parents, as to what our kids' upbringing is going to be, and there is both a freedom and a responsibility in that. My wish is that every child is given as many years as possible to enjoy the simple magic of the childhood cocoon—safe, happy, free and unencumbered by the big world that is waiting for their teen years and adulthood.

Even if you don't have kids, and no matter the age of the ones you do have, take time to incorporate some outdoor play. It does children good not only to play with adults, but to see adults play. My brothers and I delight in a good, old-fashioned round of Sardines or S-P-U-D when we get together—it is fantastic, interactive fun! And, as many of you know, I love a good excuse to be a kid again!

False Prophets

When someone of influence goes off the path of what they teach or inspire or represent, they become a false prophet. Many people, a good many children, look up to me, even idolize me, and I am not always comfortable with that because it comes with a responsibility to not only practice what I teach, but live it as my own truth, my own *dharma*.

I am very aware that if I make a choice to do something counter to what I know is my dharma, I can no longer be that prophet of inspiration to others. Is this a burden I've put upon myself? Maybe so, but I do think that's why so many we revere as our idols fail us—because they fail themselves. *They cannot see themselves as being that good*, so to them their teachings apply mainly to everyone else. Humbly I can attest, I am that good. It resonates through my energetic, spiritual being that *this is what I am here to do*. I am blessed to intuitively channel these ancient teachings for the betterment of our world. There is a simple grace to be found in living a life of faith and truth. This has challenged me to face my demons, to overcome and surrender.

In every moment of our life, we are tested to stay true to our path, our *dharma*, our truth. Look at those you admire and idolize. Hold their qualities against the mirror of your Self and know that *you* are capable of emanating those virtues. This isn't about going to church, or synagogue, or temple, it is about embracing those sacred teachings every moment of your life.

Exalted, we are all on this journey together.

The Prison of Faith

Sri Swami Satchidananda, founder and spiritual leader of Integral Yoga, believed that all faiths, all paths, lead to the One. What is faith or religion but a way in which you are uplifted, inspired to be better than you already are? At times of suffering you find comfort, love, and healing through faith. When times are good, we hold faith like a dear friend and share our joy with that god or guru. When in times of suffering or blessing, we can offer up goodness to others through Karma Yoga: selfless acts of kindness.

In Lawrence Wright's book, *Going Clear: Scientology, Hollywood, and the Prison of Belief*, I was most struck by the notion of faith being a prison and looked at what faith has cost us, how dogma can imprison us though rules and conditions, how compassion is lost, and unity gives way to "us versus them." Apparently faith in the Divine and faith in a set of human-interpreted rules are two *very* different things, and only one of them is truly spiritual.

All faiths have their place in the fabric of humanity.

Melissa Etheridge sings this sentiment so succinctly: "My god is love, my god is peace, my god loves you, and my god loves me." It seems we can be liberated in our faith after all, if we remain open to the notion that there are other people whose religion may be different, but are every bit a part of the human family as we are.

Truth Is One, Paths Are Many

I live my faith. Those attending my classes, camps, retreats or other programs experience the Light of Spirit that flows through me. I follow the Tao through *Feng Shui* and Chinese astrology. I devote myself to living the principles of Yoga philosophy, woven even into my Buddhist practice. My guru, Sri Swami Satchidananda, said, "Truth is One, paths are many."

It is true—as I walk the paths of the Tao, Buddhism, and Yoga, I no longer struggle as I once did with accommodating them all. At the heart of all faiths is a common purpose: to live for the greater good. From my sincerest understanding, that means to honor the Self, to live with an open heart embracing all living beings, to walk gently on this Earth with respect for her natural resources, to give more than I take, to live with dignity and virtue. Making the vow of the Bodhisattva—to live for the benefit of all sentient beings, that all may be free from suffering—is in many ways similar to the vow I made to my guru, to walk the path of Yoga for the sake of all people, especially children, that they may learn to live with peace of mind, ease of body, and purpose to their lives.

I grew up next door to my church, Brown Memorial Presbyterian on Park Avenue in Baltimore, Maryland. It was the foundation of my spiritual roots, and I am blessed to have many memories worshiping there for fourteen years. When my family moved as I entered high school, that was lost. I wanted so much to bring the church with me, but no one had ever taught me that God was *inside* of me and I could take him anywhere.

In my children's Yoga classes I tell them there is a crystal of Light that sits in your heart. Through meditation you can see that Light, connect to it, and let it guide you when you are lost. We all need to know that. We all need the roots of faith in our life.

I think as a nation we have lost the core values associated with living our faith. Our connection to whomever we choose to worship is founded in love and devotion for their teachings and ability to inspire us to be our best Self. It is not exclusive, like a club membership, but "all-inclusive." No matter what path of devotion you choose, we ultimately are all on the same highway and all our Paths lead to the One.

I encourage you to meditate on that crystal of Light within your heart, to breathe deeply and feel that Light radiating throughout your body, out to the world, touching all of life on this precious Earth, our shared Home.

How I Became *Nitya*

I know, in that way of knowing something without actually knowing it, that I have always been a deeply spiritual person.

As a child my religion was Nature and my church. They both inspired me and gave me a freedom of soul that I craved without realizing I was craving it. It was just something I innately gravitated toward.

There was a long, empty period of my life when I did not have a church. I had no container for my spirituality outside of my journaling, until I started my teacher training with Nora *Vimala* Pozzi through the Integral Yoga Center of Richmond. That was back in the fall of 2004. It was early December when the training took me to Satchidananda Ashram–Yogaville for a long weekend to learn Yoga philosophy from some of the swamis. I felt something twitch in me that had long been dormant.

After noon meditation one day, I was walking alone on the high road up the mountainside to Sivananda Hall for lunch. It was cool and cloudy, and as I came around the bend of the road, there the sun broke through the clouds and a chant entered me and my heart broke open. That was how I received my first mantra. That was my first heart-opening experience, there would be several more over the years. So for a long time my meditation was that mantra, using mala beads to count each recitation 108 times. It became my staff in life as I went on to graduate as a Yoga teacher, began to teach kids' Yoga, and then even branded myself as Yoga with Nitya with the release of my DVD. I learned many tough lessons during those early years of teaching.

At my graduation I received the name *Nitya*, which in Sanskrit translates to Eternal One, and couldn't imagine how I'd ever live up to such a name. Self-doubt plagued me; I wondered if I was even on the right path when so many obstacles were thrown in my way. But I persevered. I had to learn to surrender over and over again.

Then one very cold, late night in the winter of 2013, my personal life was disintegrating—my daughter was in crisis, my marriage was falling apart—and there I was in my broken-down car on the side of the road. I was hungry and cold and feeling lost in life. Quietly a mantra entered my heart and I began to chant it. A wave of comfort and acceptance of the situation rolled over me. I felt bathed in Light on that dark, dark night. It turned out to be the mantra Mahatma Gandhi chanted his entire adult life. It is a powerful mantra for healing and protection. It became my new meditation mantra. The first one, I let it go. I figured I'd graduated to the new one.

In 2017, twelve years after my first mantra found me, I was asked if I wanted to go to Yogaville to be initiated in a special ceremony for devout yogis, at which one is given a special mantra. It seemed like an auspicious time to do that. I felt that I would then have THE mantra I was meant to chant for always, and that would seal my spiritual path with my guru, Sri Swami Satchidananda. It is said the repetition of the sacred mantra is like holding the hand of your guru. It is part of the branch of Yoga called Japa, in which you invoke the blessings of the guru, of God, of the Universe, through singing or chanting their sacred names. It is not something to be taken lightly. So I began to prepare for the initiation by spending one more night chanting the mantra I'd recited for the past four years.

Then this happened . . .

As I was sitting at the altar in my living room, I lit candles, burned incense, and began to speak to *Gurudev* (my beloved guru). I shared my sorrow—even grief—at letting go of my first two mantras for the one I would be receiving the next day. I felt in that moment that I was also letting go of some of the more difficult parts of my journey and myself and was starting anew. I started to recite the old mantra as my fingers worked each of the rose quartz mala beads that I had used for so many years.

Just then, I heard a *pop*, and the mala broke in my hand. I looked at my picture of Gurudev, smiling through tears of realization. Ah, indeed the mala breaks, ending this cycle! So I chose an amethyst one to replace it, and off I went to Yogaville for initiation day, April 29th, 2017.

As I sat in the ceremony that afternoon with all the magic of ritual, I thought about the old mala beads breaking the night before, and wondered what the new mantra would be. Of the hundreds of mantras, wouldn't it be amazing if the mantra I was about to receive would be either of the ones I had already been "given?" When the time came, I was handed a little white envelope, and there inside written so lovingly *was my first mantra* plus one extra syllable. The picture of Gurudev inside the envelope was like the one on my altar.

I felt affirmed. I realized the path of this spiritual Yoga journey I had been on—with so many challenges, and setbacks, with self-doubt and questioning—was ordained from the moment I stepped on the path. I became *Nitya* before I ever had the name given to me! I have been living this name all along.

And what does it mean to be eternal? It means, for me, that like the mala beads, I am unending—no beginning or ending—just abiding in the now. I also see it as a reminder that all that I do will have an everlasting impact. This is expressed in my mission statement for teaching Nitya Living programs:

If I achieve nothing else in my life,
I hope to inspire as many children as I can
to honor themselves, to treat others with compassion,
and to love and treasure this beautiful world we all share and call
hOMe.

All that we do creates our legacy, and this holds us accountable.
Always.
Without End.
Nitya

10 Years of Teaching

April 2015 marked the 10th anniversary of my being certified as a Yoga instructor. This was a momentous and significant commemoration of the journey I have been on as I have grown into becoming *Nitya*.

That first day of teacher training was my birthday, October 21, 2004, and it came at a time in my life when I was hungry for the next step. I came by the tuition through a *Feng Shui* job in Baltimore, consulting on a strip mall that paid the exact amount that was needed. It just seemed destined to be. I can still remember walking up the steps to class and meeting Debbie *Nalini* Fazenbaker for the first time, someone who is still a dear friend and who played an essential role in my early years of teaching. True to my impulsive and passionate nature, I graduated in April, 2005, and immediately embarked on the quest to open a Yoga studio. Initially Nalini and I did this together, but after many dead ends and struggles to find a suitable location and building, I continued alone, determined to find a place. Against my own principle, to not push to make something happen when it is obviously not happening easily, I pushed—eventually finding a building on Main Street. Looking back I can see how I forced something to happen that was not meant to be at that time. The lessons I learned were beautifully painful.

I opened the doors of Just Be Yoga in the summer of 2006 with a 10-week long summer Yoga camp for kids. *Nalini* constructed the first curriculums, and in many ways taught me how to manage and run a classroom and work with children. You see, before going into this venture, I had never taught or worked with kids before. Something from within me said *this* was my path, and I was headstrong on figuring out how to make it work. We got through two incredible summer seasons at Just Be Yoga. I can still recall the opening day event, the struggle to pay the bills and fill classes, the sweet feeling of early success when I'd drive by at night and see the shoe rack full of shoes and an instructor chatting with students in the front room. My little studio on Main Street was starting to take off.

But in 2008, with the third Yoga camp season approaching, the U.S. economy collapsed. In May, Becky Eschenroeder (now a Nitya Living instructor) and I called over 60 families one afternoon, trying to fill Yoga camp, but it was not to be. Over 75% of the families were choosing other, more economical alternatives for their summer plans, as the gas prices had spiked, along with food prices, and people were being laid off from their jobs. I had no choice but to close.

The last event was a meditation program led by Swami Kenananda, from Minnesota, and afterward we sat on packing boxes and had a make-shift picnic of take-out from Sticky Rice, our favorite sushi restaurant across the street. It was as if the Universe was blessing the end of an incredibly difficult passage in my initial venture of my Yoga career. Swami Kenananda has continued to come back to Richmond to offer meditation programs.

That summer I spent at home with my daughter. It was so strange to go from being so busy and inundated with work, to having next to nothing to do but play with my girl, while redesigning how to reboot my Yoga business without Just Be. It was not easy, and in hindsight I don't think it was meant to be so. This journey I have been on has taught me so much about myself— what I am capable of, my strengths, my weaknesses, and ultimately how to live Yoga, how to live my *dharma*, my faith. Even in a Hatha Yoga class, as we move through the *asanas* or poses, we are not meant to feel comfort, we are meant to find our edge. We are to find comfort in the discomfort, to push just enough, to ride the edge until space opens up, allowing us to deepen further into the pose, into our selves, into our lives.

I can say this, I would never have made it without all the incredible children and adults who have rolled out their Yoga mats and sat before me for class, for camp, for Kirtan, and for retreats. My success is a direct result of each student's participation. My gratitude is endless. Truly, my heart swells with so much appreciation for all the people who have allowed me to give in the name of service, in the name of Yoga. There are many families who have stuck with me for the duration—little Summer was in my first toddler class; Miranda *Prasanna*, who came to my first family Yoga class at the age of four; Claudia *Vani*, who grew to be a camp counselor and lead teacher; Xavier *Guruprem*, who like my daughter, Bea *Kavita*, began at Just Be Yoga Summer Camp when they were just six. Those who started as preschoolers are now teenagers and adults, and among them was Bella *Dhyavati*, who also grew up in Yoga classes and summer camp, who illustrated my book *A Child's Journey into Yoga*. I have watched so many kids grow up. My hope is that what I have taught them has made a positive impact, a meaningful difference.

This has not just been about building a business, though some days it feels like that. It is also not always about what I could give, because, ultimately, I could not give all that I do without first having received something meaningful myself. Over these past many years I have had spiritual awakenings that cracked me wide open.

The first was during my teacher training, when we went for a long weekend to Yogaville to have teachings expounded by the swamis on Yoga philosophy. It was a cloudy gray December day just after noon meditation where I had sat in Chidambaram, the building where Sri Swami Satchidananda is entombed and a wax statue of his likeness sits prominently. I was walking alone up the high road to lunch with the chant *Om Namah Shivaya* in my mind. I may have even been singing it aloud. As I came around the bend in the road, the sun hazily shown through the clouds and struck me. Something happened to me then. I felt my heart open, *and I began to run!* I am not a runner, and I have never had much stamina for rigorous exercise, so it was bizarre to find myself running, *full speed* up the side of the mountain trail to Sivananda Hall, sobbing with joy, with release and relief. One of my colleagues was standing just outside of the woods, off the trail, when she saw me. She asked if I was okay, because I'm sure I was a sight of tears and panting and sobs. I answered, "YES!!" with full radiant joy beaming out of my heart. I was never the same after that. Something had shifted inside of me.

One night I was sitting in a large studio room leading *kirtan*, but back in those early years my confidence to sing in public was shaky. The room was filled with two dozen people. After I sang a line of a chant, the audience echoed back that line to me in the call-and-response method of *kirtan*. Their collective voices felt overwhelming, I felt myself shrinking. Then a force rose up behind me, like the great cobra rising behind Shiva's head, and this energy was like a strong hand at my back. My confidence soared and I opened my mouth to sing the next line, and there was so much power and confidence! I heard it and felt it. I knew that Gurudev had been there in that moment. My ability to lead *kirtan* grew immensely that night. Now, any time I feel any hint of insecurity with any part of leading or teaching, I summon Gurudev and he is there with me.

In June 2012, when I was in Yogaville again for a Yin Yoga teacher training with Biff Mithoefer, I had my second awakening. This time I was walking on the low road to the LOTUS shrine alone, in a very pensive place, when I reached that point in the road where the LOTUS first comes fully in view. I felt something happen to me that was indescribable at the time. When I got home, I wasn't home. For several weeks I felt like I was in two places at once. Part of me was at that spot on the road in Yogaville—I could hear people talking and walking by me as if I was still standing there—and yet, I was here in Richmond, trying to continue my everyday life. I avoided people and social activities. All I wanted to do was meditate and be alone. Then a friend advised me to not fight the feelings, to allow myself to elevate to that higher vibration of being and not try to return to the person I was before I left. They were right. In fact, after that summer my life began to change, and I went through that next year like a baptism of fire as relationships ended, and the old, last vestiges of the paradigm that had been my life fell away.

Another incredible moment came in the next years as I was again in Chidambaram in Yogaville, meditating. I had slipped into a deep meditation as I recited my mantra. Then I heard a voice in my head reciting the mantra with me. It was the voice of my guru. My heart, already open, melted into an indescribable love. I opened my eyes and looked at the wax statue of Sri Swami Satchidananda, and I smiled through tears of great bliss. I knew I would never be alone. He is in my heart for always.

There are two people who have been instrumental, and without their profound influence, I could not have arrived at this place where I am now. Foremost is my Integral Yoga teacher, Nora *Vimala* Pozzi, who pushed me so hard during the teacher training with love, with grace, with discipline, and with wisdom. The other person is someone I have never met in person, but who was at my hand as I penned my book, *A Child's Journey into Yoga*, who has had my back every time I doubted I could do what was being asked of me, whether in class or in life, and is a constant presence guiding me on this path of living Yoga with unconditional love, comfort, and support. That person is the founder and spiritual leader of Integral Yoga, Sri Swami Satchidananda, or Gurudev. I had an article published in *Integral Yoga Magazine* about Gurudev's remarkable influence on my life and my teaching.

In these first 10 years I opened and closed a studio, I transformed my car into a mobile studio, I released a kids Yoga DVD, published books, branded my name Yoga with Nitya (now Nitya Living), and started to train others to do what I do. Now I, along with other Nitya Living teachers, have taught thousands of children in day cares, schools, and studios. I have directed and run over 12 years of Yoga camp, hosted adult retreats and workshops, gone into homes for private Yoga sessions with children and adults needing specialized Yoga instruction, and I am far from finished.

At this junction I take pause and reflect, and I take pause and look forward. I am incredibly grateful, deeply moved, and motivated to grow beyond where I am now, because I see how I have inspired so many to do as Gurudev advises us to: "Be Good and Do Good."

Open the Windows

I've been in this room all day.
 Finally someone opened the windows
And the tolling bells and humming insects
 And leaves dancing floated in,
Sifting through the screen,
 And washed me in their performance.
So silent, so still am I
 That the subtlest of sounds,
Nature's whispering language,
 Translated this early evening into a mandala
 Of bells and wings and trees.
Shadows long reaching without intent,
 Simply finding their place in the web of this story.
I fold forward and sink into the silence
 To listen.

Barefoot and Breathing

The peak crests like a frothy wave and falls away.
Night descends earlier now—
Even in the heat of day there is a coolness
Lurking in the shadows.
Inhaling deeply the bounty of the garden—
Tomatoes, cucumbers, okra, basil, and thyme . . .
A volunteer sprig of dill hides
In the shade of a squash leaf.
Piles of summer's fruits fill the market stalls.
And as we reach this crescendo of season,
We inhale, waiting for the exhale of autumn—
Falling, falling with colorful song
To lay our gardens to rest.
Sweet summer's breath thick in my lungs,
Skin cinnamon-brushed by the sun's rays,
Bottoms of my feet blackened by long walks
Barefoot and breathing:
Just me, just being

Transitions

Locusts' humming vibration,
A gold finch's swooping flight,
A breeze that harbingers autumn,
The browning of the crepe myrtle trees,
A blue sky iced with thin clouds
That softens the sun's gaze.
I look out from my porch perch and listen
For what the Sages say.
"Slow down, little sister,
Slow it all down.
Plenty to do, but not all today.
Some can wait, some you can let go."
Belly round with potential,
Ripening like the moon,
I can sense changes coming,
Autumn whispers, "It'll be descending soon."
The breath is shallow,
Barely audible now.
As I sit my eyes close,
Like the clouds before the sun—
The light low.
And in this meditation, prana flutters in my veins
Like the swooping flight of the gold finch,
And I disappear into the last that remains—
The last of me Ommming a vibrant exchange of breath.
So sweet is this inner solitude whispering,
Whispering, so clearly,
"Refresh."

Shifting Seasons

The longest Indian summer
Exhaled its last
And suddenly the window of winter
Flung itself open
Tossing the final autumnal leaves
Littering them in careless piles
Around my feet
Raining golden petals
And leaving the branches bare
As if in surrender
At last, at last,
A shuddered sigh,
A raspy gasp.

I throw my mittened hands to the sky
And my eyes closed, face squinting,
See the blurry shadow
My heavily bundled self reflects
As if in surrender
At last, at last
A shuddered sigh,
A raspy gasp.

Bone cold, I sink into a hot bath
And melt into a steamy dream
As the dark descends
Upon the frost bitten garden—
Tomatoes stunted at the green
To never ripen,
Flowers folded like petaled prayers,
The hum of summer has lost its tune,

As if in surrender
At last, at last,
A shuddered sigh,
A raspy gasp.

Hands at my heart, a frozen gaze
Inhale to exhale
The vacuous sound
A season's language translated to silence.

Too Cold

A cold that digs into your bones
    Birds black as the naked trees
Pipped trilled and squawked
    Too cold for much life now
      Too cold to sit for long
    As a witness to winter

A hawk is only a raven
Through watery eyes peering
    Up into the spidery web
      Of limbs and branches

Sun licks the horizon peach
    Then sinks behind the down of clouds
Wind stings your face
    The ground is hard dry littered
      With leaves now brown

Too cold for much life now
    Too cold to sit for long
      As a witness to this winter

Don't Disturb the Disturbance

Don't disturb the disturbance—
*   Move like water with grace, with ease,*
With compassionate understanding
*   Even if you don't know.*

Don't disturb the disturbance—
*   Be patient like the bud awaiting spring*
Silent, observing, aware—
*   Even if you are ready to explode into bloom.*

Don't disturb the disturbance—
*   Like cider cloudy with sediment,*
It may not look delicious,
*   But if you let it be*
It will settle into clarity again
*   And there—you will quench your thirst.*

Don't disturb the disturbance . . .
*   Just let it be.*

Tree House

In the dark of winter, dark like
The raw umber of a moth's wings,
As the bark of the tree thickens within its casing
Infinite insects have burrowed deep to sleep.
The trunk of the tree, I imagine, is like
An apartment complex of furry animals
Housed for a season in perfect harmony.

For, don't you imagine, the tit mouse and chickadee
Commune with the squirrels,
Who nest up in the branches in a leaf dwelling
That defies gravity and sense?
Do they borrow from each other's larder?
Do they pick at the dormant insects?

And as the wind howls and bare branches bend,
All the creatures in the cavity of the tree
Trill a tune, that's more like a hum,
A sound that dissolves into the night
In somber white silence.

My Mantra

My mantra left me this morning
　In the mist of a new day rising
My two fingers rubbing the rose quartz bead
　Waiting like a breath to exhale in the rhythm
Of a familiar sound in my heart
　And it didn't come.
　　Silence.

Then it started and faltered
　Like a car engine in winter.
Instead what arose was an old sun—
　My original mantra, a forgotten friend.
We rode the mantra around
　One hundred eight times.

Then noon meditation came,
　And under the umbrella of the lotus-petaled ceiling,
My mantra came back to me,
　Dearer than before, renewing my faith,
We rode the familiar ride
　Around the mala twice.

The bells rang,
　Ending the time for silence.
The silence of my mantra rings loudly in my heart
　Be still, and know.

Breath

Breath, inhaled, runs like ice through my veins
Breath, a cloud, wordless, hovering outside my mouth
Breath, prana, life force—we collectively are one
  Breath.

Each day a new sun, each sky blooms
  With stars and clouds.
Each night a new moon, each day a blessing,
  Each moment a gift—Each breath
Breathes us further into this life.

Breath, captured in a sudden, emotional gasp;
Breath, exhaled like a kite-stringed sigh;
Breath, a beginning and ending repeated as if
  Without end.

Grateful, we pause
  Grateful, we are aware
    Grateful, we embrace
This gift, most precious—
  Right there, in here, within us, each and all
    Life.

Cupped, contained in a long sequence
  Of exquisite breaths,
Billions of them rolling,
  Like a blanket of stars through the Universe
    Of our karmic journey,
I am grateful for every one, every
  Breath.

Named Love

How could I have known my heart had fallen asleep?
*   It knew not the touch of love.*
The words of adoration fell deaf upon my ears
*   Until you woke me to this passionate youth*
So late, so late in life—but not too late.
*   Not so late that my heart couldn't melt*
*   Nor my ears delight to take in your kindness.*
I felt my soul sigh with relief, drinking in with great thirst
*   That which can only be named as Love.*

Suddenly all the years lost to drudgery and routine
*   slipped out the window,*
Lifting the dust of winter, revealing
*   The shiny wood grain of my mantle.*
A sun more radiant glows upon my cheeks now.
*   Springs blooms a more intoxicating perfume.*
Giggles alight from my mouth like bubbles
*   Of perfect luminous happiness.*

Each breath a shuddered elation—breathing,
*   Breathing so deeply*
That which can only be named as Love.

Rainbow World

The world has turned a different color,
*   One I've never known.*
I thought I knew them all,
*   But I was apparently wrong.*

It's okay, I can learn, but . . . no, this . . .
*   This color I cannot train my eyes to see*
Or my mind to comprehend.

It's okay, I can protest and refuse
*   This palette painting the landscape.*
I can choose to look away.

For I know a sky that is endless
*   With palest blue,*
Just a whisper of clouds,
*   A radiance of sunlight.*

No, that color that's spreading
*   Like ink on watery paper*
Will not bleed into that sky above me
*   Or this spirit within me.*

I choose a palette that most people agree
*   Fills a rainbow arcing the sky—*
That same sky I know—
*   Arcing our spirits like a banner*
Hung over our chests with hands at our hearts.

We sing with the birds, we run with the herds,
*   Hooves kissing the good earth.*
We swim with the finned ones, fly with the winged ones,
*   And crawl with the many legged ones.*

For those who see the colors I know,
  Know the unity our sky holds us to.
And nothing can threaten that,
  No matter how heavy the clouds,
Or violent the lightening,
  Or wrathful the storm.

That sky is there all the while, waiting,
  To be made visible once again
When we are truly ready to see.

We Are Women on Fire

We are women on fire,
Our hair an antenna to the Cosmos,
Radiating Light
To guide us forward.
Paradigm shift cracks the codes,
Breaks the known,
And casts us into the mystery
of Now.
Shadows long held reveal themselves
To be treasures,
Gifts of untold power,
For we are women on fire.

As Great Mother, we birth fertile
With vibrant Cosmic quaking force.
We are united,
Belly pressed against belly round,
Breast to heart-filled breast,
United, hands raised, hands held,
We arrive to scorch the Earth . . .

For we are women on fire.

Leaving

One after the other they flew from the tree
*   As if birthed*
But no, only from where they were perched
*   Which must have been out of view.*
The invisible, discordant trills and tunes
*   Layer my hearing*
With car engine accelerations,
*   And the incessant woodpecker-like hammering*
*   Of construction blocks away.*
Then, in a gasping gush, a roar of wings!
*   They lift up as if on cue,*
And they chorus into the sky—
*   An ink-blotted cloud once there,*
*   And then again gone.*
And the world is no quieter for their leaving.

Prematurely Empty-Nested

They leave traces behind
  Like fake blood from Halloween on the porch railing—
    Oh, what a mess that was!
  And the fingerprints smeared a dingy gray
    along the stairwell walls,
  And the empty glass by the bed—
    The bed they left in balled up sheets
      and pillows piled high.

They leave us and they return to us
  Like a compulsive string pulling at our hearts
    Out of our own rhythm,
      On their own terms,
  Or just, as it happens to be,
    Discordant, unpredictable life.

The challenge, I suppose then, is to find a tune
  In the strings that play
And attempt to enjoy it enough
  That the returning is better
Than the inevitable leaving
  That starts as soon as they arrive.

Heron Totem

A line along the horizon
Moving to a methodical beat of the wing—
Like breath, slow and pulsed—
In search of a watery place
To land and roam
And hunt and rest.

The heron stands
Like upright driftwood,
A line in the sand,
An eye cutting through the river—
watching, waiting, selecting,
And timing is everything.
Wrapped in a silent pulse of patience,
Moving in rhythm to the river's current,
The push of the wind, the pull of the moon.

And then up again
With a powerful beat of the wings
Long and blue and gray.
A feathered gust, a tortured cry—
Why such an unforgiving voice
Given to one so full of grace?
Yet, like the piercing scream of the hawk,
They call us to look up.

And in seeing out to the winged line
Moving in the sky,
We look within, feel our own pulse,
Hear our own scream,
Find our own grace,
And we fly.

By Lantern Light

By lantern light,
  Tibetan prayers I chant
Through the rattle and blast
  Of a train miles away.
Outside my tent,
  Deer have gathered.
As I walk the path,
  We look at each other.
There in that moment
  Fear and love,
The duality of all of life,
  Flows together and is one.
As the train whistle blows
  Its insistent breath,
Birds on the wing
  Lift up the new day.
By lantern light
  I discover mine.
By lantern light,
  The path illumines.
I rise.

Edge of Living

And there you were—
 Beautiful, raw, on the precipice,
Shaking down to the marrow,
 Licking the wound of some
Unknown tomorrow.

And if you leapt, who's not to say
 Someone would pull you back
And hold you here,
 Crying out how much you're needed.
How we are all stymied by fear!

And there we are, standing—
 Not realizing our eyes are closed,
Breathing and yet not smelling
 The fragrance inhaled by our own nose,
Wrapped in a shroud we deny exists,
 Cursing all that happens,
As some cruel karmic-fated twist.

And yet, to open our eyes—
 To breathe the breath of flowers—
To fully engage in our lives,
 To simply self-empower,
Is that very cliff's edge we kiss.

Let us not hold back
 Or get lost in an ignorant mist,
But surrender into the bliss
 That life is such
An incredible gift.

Seeds and Dreams

Under the filling moon I saw them,
The first sprouts rising up,
Misted and sparkling like gems.
What grows in this garden of my heart,
Unleashed in dreams, creased on the pillow,
Pressed and fresh come morning?
And like a child anxious to open a gift,
I run to the window to see what the night grew
Under that white-lighted moon.
I'm still looking, I'm still searching
For what grows out of dreams
Inspired by memories.
I go outside and my feet are wet with grass and clover dew.
I dig my fingers into the earth and breathe
My first full, fertile breath—
An inhalation like roots expanding,
Exhaling stars and seeds.

Soundless Words

All my words fell out of my mouth
*   And scattered in the garden.*
Snapdragons roared
*   And burned some up.*
Inside the squash blossoms
*   the orange-yellow of a bee*
Bouncing about, covered in pollen
*   And tipsy, as if drunk*
*   On its own buzz.*
I kneel as if in prayer,
*   As if this space were as sacred*
As it is, perhaps.
*   Each season mulched over*
And over again
*   Like a memory replayed*
Over and over again.
*   Seasons, moon cycles,*
Time's strange undulating passage
*   Slowly revealing wisdoms—*
Soundless words
*   I strain to decipher.*

Honey Fingerprints

It's messy sweet like honey.
Chewing the raw ginger
At the bottom of my tea cup,
The sharp burning bite splinters
Down my throat and is then coated
By the warm drip of honey,
   Soothed.

All of my days I pull the strings
Of my interactions and responsibilities
Like a thread as fine as a spider's web—
Fragile and strong and purposeful.
I speak my truth, I stand strong in the current
And walk into the deepest waters
   Only to find them shallow . . .
The illusion of our challenges.

I am my true, authentic Self,
Rooted as a mighty oak
Or a weeping cherry tree
Raining blossoms
In the wind of my words.
If you pay attention the answers are there,
   Messy as sweet honey fingerprints.

The Journey Home

Stretch long like a wing unfurled.
Catch the wind of flight.
Soar on the currents of breath.
Where are you?
Are you here?
Have you always been?
To see your Self, close your eyes,
And the mirror reflects perfectly
All that is you.

Can you see? Have you always seen?
Through tears you'll remember
Joy unbridled.
Through hurt, you'll remember
The soothing sense of pleasure.
Through anger you'll breathe
Towards calm.
Through loneliness you'll reach
And find your own hand . . .
Hold on.

Roll out your mat; see it as a path
You wear down until it is worn through—
Pilled, pitted, holey.
Where are you on this journey?
Have you always wandered
And wondered?
If you are present in this Now
You will see your True Self
Clearly reflected before you.

As the path of your mat blooms
With 10,000 lotus blossoms
You will weep
With profound deep blissful relief,
That for all your wandering and wondering,
You have finally come hOMe.

Searching for Home

A shift moves us forward
  And what was a now
    Becomes past.
Memories gathered into times
  That lie crisp and fresh in our minds—
    For now. For now.
And with a sigh weighted
  With all the decisions that brought us here,
    We step into the future
Unknown with trepid hope
  And courage and curiosity,
    To come to the realization
      One day . . . one day
All those memories we held so dear
  Will have moved off into the distance
    Like a heron along the horizon,
Seeking new waters, sinking his long toes
  Into the murky shoreline,
    Scanning for new territory.
We are all searching
  For home. For home.

Seedling

An idea takes shape—
A seed in the mind,
Pregnant with possibility—
A future seen, but not here,
Yet.
Then it's lost, forgotten
Amongst the fabric of days
Tethered to so much doing,
But then,
But then something—
A message, a sign, an introduction
Reignites the dormant seed
And it swells into a bud.
From the pit of the stomach
An intuitive voice calls to the mind,
"Remember."
The urge to push
Mounts into a scream of necessity
To manifest.
No room for doubt
Or postponements,
Or procrastination.
It is here—Now.
Now is the time
To be birthing.

Daffodils

Two boys biking.
  Daffodils sunning on the lawn.
A man with a ladder looks up
  Into the tree of his work.
Someone enters a shop
  With a bell's ring
To buy something
  Useless.
A hawks' cry
  Pierces the warming air.
Its mate answers
  Devotedly.
And two boys are biking.
  Their laughter is lost in the din of the day;
Their afternoon is open and endless
  As childhood can be.
So simply, so simply,
  Two friends.
And even now, somehow,
  Nothing else matters.

The Elephant in the Room

Somehow, this year,
The anniversary of that terrible day
Passed by unnoticed.
Maybe enough time has passed.
Maybe it's a sign of healing,
Of forgiveness, of trust.

Sometimes life takes us to the edge
Of all we know, of all we are,
With no direction seeming possible,
That no scream to the sky can swallow and assuage.

We fall into the unknown
Where the answers echo in our bones
Telling us to live through it,
Breathe, breathe it in. Hold it there—
Hold it close and feel that edge on your skin,
Just like she did.

All you know is teetering in discomfort, waiting
To wake up, to wake us up slightly changed,
Like the way the light shifts in the room
When the seasons change and shadows
Are either lifted or fall longer,
When some things once darkened are illuminated
Or are suddenly lost.

So this year, we went past the anniversary,
This event that could've been marked with stones.
Over and over we surrender
To all we know, to all we are, and somehow . . .
Somehow, she is still here.
That is the elephant in the room.

The Onion

A young man had a fine garden behind his cottage. He had enjoyed the bounty of his garden for many years. One day a terrible storm rolled in over the mountains and brought torrential rains to his valley. All of his garden was washed into the road. He watched helpless and in deep anguish. Many thoughts filled his mind and his sorrow deepened. The night fell and he collapsed in despair.

The morning brought a fresh new day, but all around the cottage the man saw his beautiful valley destroyed—trees had fallen, roofs had peeled off of homes, and crops washed away. Even though the young man's home was intact, all he could see was his empty garden, once so rich with vegetables that would feed him through the winter. He knelt down and wept on the wet ground. Through his tear-filled eyes he saw something in the soggy earth, a glistening skin of an onion, a big round onion like a pearl. He took the onion inside and put it on a clean, round plate. He could never bring himself to eat it. As the days passed all he saw in the onion was the memory of the destruction of his lost garden.

On the seventh day after the storm, an old monk came by with his morning begging bowl. The young man opened his door, and upon seeing the monk's bowl, laughed with irony. The young man showed the monk his own empty bowl and then pointed towards his barren garden. The monk smiled and invited the young man to join him on his walk. The monk listened as the man told of the terrible storm and his anguish over the loss of his garden.

After a long while the two men came to the bank of a very wide river. There was a small wooden boat tied to a stake. The monk gestured to the young man to get into the boat. The man began to argue with the monk, "Why should I come with you? Why do you want me to leave my home?" The monk replied, "You told me how this storm destroyed your garden, but I have also heard through your story how this storm destroyed your spirit. I saw a big, white onion on your table. You might have used it to make a nice broth, but you left it there to rot in your cottage, which was not damaged at all by the storm."

The monk unmoored the boat and eased it into the river. He turned to the young man and said, "I am taking you to a place where you can heal from your loss and find new meaning in your life." The monk reached his hand out to him saying, "Please join me."

So the two men began to cross the river in the little boat. A storm suddenly came up and the young man panicked, fearing for his life. He relived all the anguish from the night of the other storm and his mind went wild. He felt trapped in this little boat in the middle of the river. He stood up pulling at his hair, his eyes wild, and the boat rocked perilously. All the while the monk sat quietly with a calm smile on his face. The man sat down breathless with his emotions and then considered diving into the rough waters and drowning himself.

Eventually, somehow, the boat managed to cross to the other shore and the sun broke through the blackened clouds. As the men stepped out of the boat the monk turned to the young man and asked, "Have you crossed the river now?"

The young man looked deeply into the old monk's eyes and began to weep. As he looked back across the river he saw the distance he had come was not nearly as far as it had felt. His tears ran freely and soon he smiled, feeling a warm glow spreading through his chest. The monk smiled too, and said, "Often in life we are forced to cross rivers in order to grow. Some people tip the boat over and drown. Others row back to where they started and never make it across. But some do cross the river and find liberation. I am glad you chose to cross the river."

The young man turned to pull the boat ashore, and upon turning back, the old monk was gone. Where the monk had stood there on the sand sat a clean, round plate that held one large white onion that shone like a pearl. The young man knelt down and said with a grateful heart, "This will make a fine broth."

A Dear Bird

In the mourning
It begins even before the dusk of death
When the body meets its final illness
You know
You know what comes
Just as sure as the sun rises
A reminder of those long since gone
All the days passed and passing
The luminous yellow feathers
A flight of sunlight
So soft against the skin
Rays of light, billows of breath
The sound of bird feet on the hardwood floors
The sound of a voice that is all but song
Whistling a lilting, happy tune
Eyes closed, breath slows, a hush floats
Like a stray feather hovering in the static air
Dawn lifts the veil of darkness
Revealing a morning of mourning
A feathered friend flying
So far, so far out of sight
Yet never closer
To the nest you made of my heart

FOR LOONY

Pebble Smoothed

Be gentle, be kind—
Life travels us along enough rough roads.
Like the rock breaking the stream,
Forcing the water to change course.
What obstructs you?
What has said there is no passage here?
Are you on a detour, have you lost your way,
Or reclaimed your own path?
Be tempered, be humble—
Let time tumble you, smooth you like a pebble.
So many pebbles rubbed so very small,
Like a beach of countless grains—
Seemingly insignificant.

Have you found your place?
Have you felt the impact of your purpose?
Are you just wandering or has gratitude reminded you
To step into your light?
For no one is any less than—
Look at the sky, so many stars.

Wonder

Like a lightning bug flickering in your heart,
  There is a joyfulness, a light
That, even in its diminutiveness,
  Diminishes the shadows
Like the child of summer
  Filled with the wonder of hot night insects.
The firefly bounces inside the jar
  Your heart has become,
Contained and longing for freedom.

Trust then that the tiniest of lights
  Can delight those that are seeking
To cast off the darkness shadowing their souls.
  A million stars, a million fireflies,
Magical luminescence
  Lighting and languid
As it falls dark, then sparks again.

Love of a Tree

The sidewalk pitches and cracks
Under the immense roots of a tree
Growing out of the concrete.
So obviously was the tree here first,
Simply by her great mass.
I have stopped here on countless walks,
Even altered my route for another chance
To stand with her,
To place my hand on her weathered skin,
And breathe with her,
To look up into the perfect chaos of her branches
With great reverence
As I imagine her network of roots
unseen,
But felt
By the neighboring trees who share her pulse.

Woodpecker

Red headed great god bird
  Hammerhead hammering
Knocking a message into the tree
  Into me—
Listen, what does she say?
  Listen, listen . . .
She's flown away

Once I saw her in the woods,
  Her flight crossed my path,
Her red head disappeared
  Into the cool, humid shadows

I strained to hear her working
  on another tree:
Knock, knock, knocking
  A message into me

I Am but a Tree

I am but a tree with roots digging deep,
  Deep down in the Earth,
And she holds me there.
  My roots hold hands with her soil and stones.

I am an ant living in the bark of the tree
  From a colony that has been here
For as long as the tree has been.
  We are a community interdependent.

I am a heron with a rookery
  Of other herons, living and nesting
In this one big, old tree.
The river feeds us, the branches circled
  With feathers, mud, and twigs
    Are our home.

  Tree = Mother Earth
  Ant = Community
  Heron = Family

Are any of us anything without the other?
How could there be a world without trees,
  Without insects, without birds,
    Without us?
We survive by the gifts of Mother Earth,
  By our global community,
    By the foundations set by our families.

But ultimately we must ask:
  Why am I here?
Is it to connect to all of it?
Is it to find meaning, derive purpose,
  Make an impact, however insignificant?

I am the tree.
  I am the ant.
    I am the heron.

I am Mother Earth.
  She is me.

From a Dream

I have a strength that puts people off,
*   Some people.*
Instead of feeling powerful, I feel awkward.
I can be that great wave that washes people clean,
*   That purifies, and in-lightens.*

Some people are ready. They find me
*   And I hold their tears in a cup*
*   So we can look at them together.*
We hold them,
*   Then throw them back to the ocean.*

I am the culmination of many—
*   The journey I'm on has many footprints.*
Despite feeling lonely, I know I am never alone.
Surely, one day, the light that I am
*   Will not seem so glaring,*
But will be seen as gentle illumination.

A strong woman should not be a threat,
*   But a comfort.*
Just as the tsunami crests,
*   I take a breath into the wave,*
*   Am pulled into its belly—down under—*
*   And it turns into snow.*

I exhale. I exhale.
The ocean is a blanket of white—
*   Its depths unknown, hidden—*
Like me, quieted down,
*   But deep.*

Breathe

Change is the point at which we have a choice to grow.
Embracing – Surrendering – Allowing
This very now moment is the seed from which
The next moment connects.
In the darkness of the unknown
Breathe – Release
In the dawning light of acceptance
Breathe – Embrace
Open your eyes and step out into the day
With the wonder of a child.
Recognize the breath you breathe
Is the same air or wind that moves through all life,
Throughout the world, connecting and holding us
In the arms of the Universe

Breathe

Sweet Nectar

The fullness of life is sweet nectar.

One of the most powerful, meaningful moments
  is when we put a seed in the ground,
Nurture it, watch it grow, eat its fruits, can the leftovers,
  and save the seeds for next year.
The raw, primal connection of human being
  and Mother Earth.
It's dirt-under-the-nails kind of happy.
And even if there is no harvest,
  even if bugs devour the crop,
    even if the sun scorches and no rain falls,
      still there is so much virtue in trying.

I put a seed in the ground with the hopes
  that it would blossom me,
    nurture me, as I nurtured it.
But really, I was fed the moment I put my hands on Her,
  Inhaled Her fertility,
And dug into Her
  to plant a single, tiny seed.

The fullness of life is sweet nectar.

Iris

Her name is Iris.
  She is in first grade.
She is a spunky little girl,
  A willow bending with innocence and mirth,
And like most kids, when the opportunity arises,
  Mischievous.

I teach hundreds of kids.
  This is one of the ones I remember—
Not for who she is—
  But for what she represents.
Iris resembles my childhood friend.
  Her name is Tracy.
We met at my second birthday party
  In 1968.
As a child she was spry, sturdy,
  Ready for an adventure,
    Ready to question authority,
      and speak her truth.

When I first met Iris
  My heart leapt in its ribbed cradle.
I saw a little girl I knew so long, long, long ago—
  Freckled, pug-nosed, a bob of brown hair with bangs
    Neatly cutting into her deep brown eyes.
I wanted to confess to Iris what she meant to me,
  All that her presence fills me with,
But she couldn't know . . .
  She couldn't possibly comprehend how desperately
A middle-aged woman would want to experience again
  Something as magical as a childhood friend.

A Hypocrite's Ode to a Tree

Who knows how many decades
They grew together
In neighboring yards?
Below the surface, running deep,
Their roots intertwined
And became their path of communication.
What do trees say to each other?
What secret, earthen language connects them
In their underground world?

On this day, this bright spring day,
The chain saws started up, and
Hour,
by hour,
by hour
They dismantled the tree I could see best
From my bedroom window.
The wood chipper ground up its flesh
To be laid under bushes and around trees in another yard
As mulch.

The countless unknown communities
That called this tree a home
Are now gone.
No one knocked on the door to tell them to move out—
These men came without warning,
Wielding their weapons of destruction.
The neighboring tree in the next yard over,
Hung her branches low,
Her leaves seemed to darken.

I could feel her grief.
　　I could feel her roots recoiling.
　　　In my window perch I wept with her.
Finally I could take it no more;
　　I ran down and wrapped my arms around her.
　　　"I'm sorry," I whispered.
Could she still feel the echo of her friend's energy fading?
　　Could she feel its pain?
　　　Was there pain?

I hugged her closer.
　　"Thank you for being here."
　　　My words felt hollow.
Such a hypocrite—I am writing on paper.
　　I'm writing on rolled out, pressed, and lined
　　　Tree flesh.
My pen is a chain saw.

　　"I'm sorry."

Anonymous

The train skims over the surface of the deep, dark water
   Unnamed
Like the passenger, next to me
   Sharing this journey.
In the silence of the car I hear all the human sounds—
   Sniffles, sighs, mumbling conversations
      Unknown.

I myself am one of the anonymous in this collective,
   Rocked and jostled through landscapes—
Bleeding light and trees pinned against a swath of blue sky
   And foaming clouds,
The peaks of rooftops and tattooed concrete buildings
   Unclaimed—
The business names faded,
   Unreadable.

I watch out the window for the next glide over water—
   Everything so flat,
So nameless,
   So anonymous,
      So perfectly not still.

A Rainy Day Musing

On a rainy day I feel called from my desk
  To sit in the rocking chair—
The same rocking chair my mother rocked me in.
  I sit looking out into the gray, fuzzy morning.
I cradle my warm cup of tea,
  Tea that a friend gave me.
    Each sip keeps me company.

One dog lies on a silk pillow my mother made
  From fabric another friend gave me—
A friend who has long since moved away.
  I miss her company.
The other dog is draped over the back of the couch,
  Having given up on chasing squirrels for today.

Not a bird trills, not a creature scurries,
  And the deer I saw last night are hunkered down
    In spirals of soggy grass.
We are all waiting for the sun to return;
  We are all waiting for a day not like today,
    and yet
This is the day we have.

There is a quiet blessing to being home—
  To witness the silence of rain on the window,
The slippered steps shuffling on the hardwood floors,
  And the sighing breaths—
When you've rocked yourself to sleep
  In the rocking chair.

The Language of Silence

When I learned the language of silence,
I was but a child—
Seen, not heard.
When I found my voice it was a language
Of rage and blame,
And I was lost.
Now my voice has quieted—
It can be a whisper;
It can be silence,
For I've learned the most powerful language.

In my solitude, I delight in silence,
For it is from that vast wellspring
That so much creativity bubbles up,
So much wisdom is learned,
And healing happens.
If you are going to speak,
Make it meaningful and necessary.
Silence is a language we must all learn to speak.
In silence all languages are heard,
All voices are tuned to the One
In which everything is birthed
And made manifest.

As the seasons mellow into autumn,
And then the hush of winter,
A sweet spot opens in the throat that longs to speak
The language of snow fall, the sound of leaves
Breaking from the bough,
The greatest perfection of expression.
For in silence everything is said in nothing at all.

Evening Remembrances

i

The sun kissed my shoulders.
The ocean danced with my feet.
The wind laughed through my hair.
The salt and sand became my skin.
I felt my heart pounding with the surf.

I went to the ocean and found myself there.

ii

Riding home as the sun sank low in the sky
  Grazing the corn-checkered farmland,
First in a golden honey glow,
  Then sweet rose.
To look back down the road from where I'd just come,
  To see the last of the sun drink itself in a
    Tangerine song.
Crystal in my fist;
  The night lying up ahead.
Deer find safety in the shadows
  On the edge of the woods beyond the field.
I see them.
  It is time to graze.

Frog's Leap

I've never been one to shy away from an idea
  Or a spontaneous inspiration.
Leaping forward with the buoyant enthusiasm of a frog,
  I've found myself face-planted time and again
    On the lily pad of life,
Wet, stung, and rejected.
  ... Or was it ejected?

No matter. I keep going.
  I keep swimming into the channel.
Deep,
  Deep
    Is the pull of the undertow I wrestle against
      As it tries to pull me down.
But I resiliently rise,
  Swimming to the surface.

Frog stroke.

Abiding with the One

I sit down and a stream of sacred names floods my mind.

I want to sing them all—
  all the chants,
    all the prayers—
From all the days of walking so many paths.

They have all led me to the One, the one home
  Here with my beloved Gurudev.

Here my heart abides, at peace.

Perhaps the greatest surrendered journey is the one
in which there is no path at all.

Lydia *Nitya* Griffith at her home in Richmond, Virginia

Made in the USA
Columbia, SC
14 June 2018